ERNEST HEMINGWAY

Modern Literature Monographs

○○○(

ERNEST HEMINGWAY

Samuel Shaw

Frederick Ungar Publishing Co.
New York

Copyright © 1973 by Frederick Ungar Publishing Co., Inc.
Printed in the United States of America
Library of Congress Catalog Card No.: 78-134827
ISBN: 0-8044-2823-9 (cloth)

Contents

Chronology

1899: Ernest Hemingway is born at Oak Park, Illinois, on 21 July.

1917: Graduates from Oak Park High School. Takes a job as reporter on the Kansas City *Star*.

1918: Volunteers as ambulance driver with Red Cross. Is assigned to Italian war theater. Receives severe wounds at Fossalta.

1919: Returns home from the war.

1920: Takes a job as feature writer for the Toronto *Star Weekly*.

1921: Marries Hadley Richardson. Goes to Paris with her.

1923: *Three Stories and Ten Poems* is published in Paris.

1924: *in our time* is published in Paris.

1925: Begins a friendship with Scott Fitzgerald. *In Our Time* is published by Boni and Liveright.

1926: *The Torrents of Spring* and *The Sun Also Rises* are published by Charles Scribner's Sons.

1927: Divorces Hadley, and soon after marries Pauline Pfeiffer. *Men without Women* is published.

1928: Makes his first visit to Key West, Florida. Hemingway's father commits suicide.

I

○○○

Nihilism
and the
American
Dream

In Hemingway's "The Snows of Kilimanjaro," Harry, the central character, is lying ill on an African plain. In the course of a hunting expedition a carelessly treated scratch on his knee has turned gangrenous. The infection has spread to his thigh; death is near. With the waiting buzzards as observers, Harry knows that he is dying. He has no patience with the efforts of his wife to reassure him:

"You're not going to die."

"Don't be silly. I'm dying now. Ask those bastards." He looked over to where the huge, filthy birds sat, their naked heads sunk in the hunched feathers. A fourth planed down, to run quick-legged and then waddle slowly toward the others.

"They are around every camp. You never notice them. You can't die if you don't give up."

"Where did you read that? You're such a bloody fool."

Hemingway saw himself and all humanity in Harry's situation—death sits with us from the beginning of life—and like Harry he refused the solace of fine words, lofty sentiments, and spiritual clichés. When Harry asks where Helen had read the old saw about not giving up, both Harry and Hemingway are rejecting the genteel tradition in American life, especially in literature, that had popularized and vulgarized the American Dream. In nineteenth-century America people were hooked on spiritual hallucinogens. Hemingway would attempt to play it straight; he would try for the truth. In his view, the human condition was essentially tragic: defeat and frustration were built into the very structure of life. Popular literature and Sunday sermons might tell Americans that hard-working people inevitably rose to affluence, that bootblacks became millionaires and dedicated their fortunes to the im-provement of mankind, that all true lovers finally were joined in everlasting marriage. For Hemingway, how-ever, as he concluded in *Death in the Afternoon,* "there is no remedy for anything in life."

The spirit of nihilism—the denial of any objective basis for truth, especially moral truth—constitutes the background for Hemingway's vision. In Europe, ni-hilism had been identified and analyzed in the nine-teenth century by Nietzsche and Dostoyevsky. Based as it was on the erosion of the classical and Christian foundations of Western civilization, the nihilist position was essentially pessimistic. The depth of the European cultural tradition, however, softened the harsh outlines of nihilism. Nietzsche ends in an ecstatic affirmation of life; Dostoyevsky, in a plea for an existential leap into religious belief. Both men found their way back to the tradition after cutting away its rational underpinning.

When the nihilist spirit reached America in the twentieth century it assumed a truculence that was a reaction to the gentility of nineteenth-century Ameri-can culture. One thinks of Robert Ingersoll challenging God to strike him dead. There is something naive and daringly adolescent in the American form of nihilist thought. In Europe nineteenth-century writing had prepared the way for the shock of Nietzsche. Novelists like Balzac and Flaubert had analyzed in depth the shortcomings of bourgeois society. In America, the op-timism of an Emerson or a Whitman offered no effec-tive cushion for the shock. Writers like Hawthorne and Melville, who saw the darker side of the American ex-perience, still expressed their vision in genteel prose. It was writing in the spirit of Sunday rather than of workaday Monday. Mark Twain, in retrospect, came to grips with the realities of American life, but in his own time he was accepted only as a humorist and entertainer.

Hemingway reflects a stark, often rhetorical nihilism with some of the angry tones of midwestern populism. In America, after the disillusionment with the war to save the world for democracy, it was impossible to use the old foundations to justify the popular philosophic and moral verities. The underside of American life was exposed for examination. The muckrakers— Lincoln Steffens, Ida Tarbell, and Samuel Hopkins Adams, among others—had begun even earlier to expose the seamy side of American economic and social life. In fiction William Dean Howells, Theodore Dreiser, and Upton Sinclair had already presented American life with some of the rosiness filtered out. Dreiser's Sister Carrie does not suffer the torments of conscience when she becomes a "fallen" woman, nor does she inevitably slide into the life of a prostitute. In the cities of America, survival was enough of a problem to make irrelevant the moral clichés of the past.

After Charles Lyell, Darwin, Marx, and Freud, the easy answers are gone. Dostoyevsky's Ivan Karamazov knows what has happened to the world when he observes that if God is dead, everything is permitted. If life and death have no transcendent significance, if man is made in the image of an ape, how do we determine what is moral and what immoral?

Hemingway does not approach the problem as a philosopher. If he reflects the spirit of nihilism, it is because he breathed the air of America. The malaise was there, the sudden awareness of Adam after he ate the apple. One did not need to pick it up in a college lecture hall. Hemingway, whose formal education never went beyond high school, remained antiacademic and antiintellectual all his life. He always preferred the thing to the theory. His origins are closer to American experience than to literary reflections of that experience.

The recognition of nothingness, *nada*—the loss of ultimate meaning in life—is Hemingway's starting point. In *A Farewell to Arms*, Frederic Henry, a volunteer ambulance driver in the World War I Italian army expressed uneasiness before high-sounding phrases that cannot be believed in:

> I was always embarrassed by the words sacred, glorious, and sacrifice and the expression in vain. We had heard them, sometimes standing in the rain almost out of earshot, so that only the shouted words came through, and had read them, on proclamations that were slapped up by billposters over other proclamations, now for a long time, and I had seen nothing sacred, and the things that were glorious had no glory and the sacrifices were like the stockyards at Chicago if nothing was done with meat except to bury it. There were many words that you could not stand to hear and finally only the names of places had dignity.

Modern men, young people most of all, find that Hemingway speaks to them in his rejection of the glorious phrases and in his recognition that the ideal by which we live often stands forth as hypocrisy when measured by what actually is. Of course this recognition is somewhat too easy in both Hemingway and the youth of the contemporary counterculture. The precise relationship between the ideal and the actual is complex. For example, Frederic Henry's thoughts on high-sounding words may just as easily be applied to the war against Hitlerism, with obviously less validity. As Hemingway came to realize in his maturity, moral positions may draw us into immoralities.

Hemingway was clearly in violent reaction to nineteenth-century American idealism. The optimism of an Emerson or a Whitman made him blush. The life Hemingway saw was brutal and degrading.

How to live then? What to do with one's life? For one thing, Hemingway did not reject life itself; a man may enjoy experience even if he can find no firm philosophic anchor. By temperament he was a man who appreciated the good things of life. There were spectacles to be enjoyed, whiskey to be drunk, women to be loved. There were forests to be camped in, streams with trout to be caught, snow on the mountains, pure air to breathe, and cool dry nights when sleep comes easy. As the existentialist Ivan Karamazov said it, one may love life more than the meaning of life.

Love of life in Hemingway, however, is accompanied by an acute awareness of *nada*. The smell of death suffuses his writing. Hemingway's obsession with death is expressed in most of his works. In several instances, his anguish overflows into the artistic creation and results in a personal confession. In *A Farewell to Arms* Frederic's ruminations during his reunion with Catherine in a hotel give the reader the impression that Hemingway is himself talking:

I know that the night is not the same as the day: that all things are different, that the things of the night cannot be explained in the day, because they do not then exist, and the night can be a dreadful time for lonely people once their loneliness has started. But with Catherine there was almost no difference in the night except that it was an even better time. If people bring so much courage to this world the world has to kill them to break them, so of course it kills them. The world breaks every one and afterward many are strong at the broken places. But those that will not break it kills. It kills the very good and the very gentle and the very brave impartially. If you are none of these you can be sure it will kill you too but there will be no special hurry.

There has been considerable speculation on the relationship between Hemingway's fiction and his life. Philip Young's critical-biographical *Ernest Hemingway* asserts that the obsession with death in Hemingway's work is traceable to the shock occasioned by the serious wounds suffered by him during his service with the Italian army in World War I.

In much of Hemingway's fiction it is easy to identify real people who served as models. On several occasions the individuals in question reacted angrily to the assumed portraits. Hemingway drew heavily on people and incidents from his own experience, as most writers do. The precise relationship between life and art, however, can never be pinned down. Everything is subject to the writer's artistic vision since the work of art, from one point of view, lives a life of its own.

By his own admission, Hemingway wrote about what he had actually experienced. Most of his fiction is obviously close to the events of his life. It is a mistake, however, to view Hemingway's fiction as autobiography. One must always keep a distance between the work of art and the artist's life, although that distance is infinitely varied and infinitely complex. In a sense, a writer appears in all his fictional characters and in none. One may read "The Snows of Kilimanjaro" as a confessional story and go very wide of the mark.

Artistic truth clearly is concerned with life truth, but that is about all one can safely say. Hemingway's "truth" was not a mere transcript of his life. In his introduction to *Men at War*, a collection, edited by him, of great battle scenes from European and American literature, Hemingway declared that "a writer's job is to tell the truth," and that his imagination, based on his own experience, "should produce a truer account than anything factual can be." In his aesthetics Hemingway was close to Aristotle's concept of the probable. His aim was universal truth.

The first requirement for the Hemingway hero is freedom from illusions. He must know the score on life and death, and he must not discuss that score openly. He must be stoic in the losing battle; he must not be afraid. From this position Hemingway developed an approved code of behavior. One does not make a fuss about things or behave clumsily, one drinks heavily but does not get drunk, one loves but does not seek possession. The big-game hunter, the athlete, the good soldier, especially the bullfighter, became for Hemingway ideal representations of the man who lives with death but does not overdramatize himself. He has guts, which Hemingway defined as "grace under pressure." It is this code that leaves Hemingway open to caricature—the code hero as a combination of Tarzan and Wild Bill Hickok with headquarters at Club 21.

There is more in Hemingway, however. His nihilism, which may even have included an element of posturing, was always at war with his compassion and romanticism. His heart sought and *wanted* to believe in something more, something that made the game worth playing. He finally came to an essentially tragic affirmation of life, as affirmative and tragic as contemporary Americans are apparently capable of accepting. Hemingway is the prototype of the nay-sayer who, one suspects, loves his fellowmen, even his country, more than he will allow himself to express. When he says something good about humanity he finds it necessary to conclude with something like "and all that sort of jazz."

Since even Emerson and Whitman were turned to use by high-riding American capitalism, the disillusioned modern cannot talk like them. Nevertheless, he continues to pick out of their words and ideas what can be presented as a revolt. From his earliest youth Hemingway was drawn to the life close to nature. He loved hunting and fishing at Walloon Lake in northern Michigan, where his family had a summer cottage. This is Thoreau on a part-time basis, peculiarly enough not unlike the life style of the businessman who must periodically get away from it all by leaving business, home, and family for communion with unspoiled nature. Americans are closer than they imagine to Huckleberry Finn, for whom happiness is an escape from civilization; floating down the Mississippi on a raft is closer to Eden than is a schoolroom or an office.

The American Dream embodied the desire to keep life simple, to stay clear of the pretentious and the ossified, to somehow avoid the straitjackets of Europe. The dream has remained even as America has gone down the path of industrialization, urbanization, and mechanization. Hemingway's work reflects both tendencies. He loved the American Dream even when he found it in a Spanish mountain stream or an African game preserve. He detested the economics and mechanization of America, yet he was at home with the cultural excrescences of industrial America—its sophistication, its barrooms, its worship of success. If he was Huck Finn, he was Huck Finn with a bankroll and the intention of returning to the Paris bistros.

Hemingway, shorn of illusions, still had to grapple with the problem of morality. In *Death in the Afternoon* he said that "what is moral is what you feel good after and what is immoral is what you feel bad after." This quotation has often been cited as proof of Hemingway's nihilism and hedonism. It sounds tough and honest in its simplicity, but one must ask the inevitable question—how long after? Hemingway surely appreciated immediate physical pleasure, but he did not stop with it. He upheld political, moral, and spiritual values requiring self-sacrifice and commitment to high ideals. In his last books Hemingway came close to affirming transcendental values and an asceticism of sorts.

Even in Hemingway's earliest successful novel, *The Sun Also Rises*, the promiscuous Brett Ashley gives up Pedro Romero, her matador lover, because she feels that she is not good for him. She tells Jake, whose love for her has been made impossible of fulfillment by his emasculation through a war wound, that "It makes one feel rather good deciding not to be a bitch. . . . It's sort of what we have instead of God." Hemingway's tough moral measure is closer to the idea of the Christian conscience and the inner check than one would first think. In this respect he is very much like Henry James, one of his favorite novelists.

Byron's Don Juan said that he laughed at mortal things to keep himself from weeping; Hemingway understates so that he will not weep. His characters feel more deeply than they are willing to say or Hemingway to make explicit. Hemingway's embarrassment with "fine" language, and his unwillingness to expatiate on spiritual states, are literary manifestations of the modern rejection of didacticism and sentimentality. Underneath the firm, muscular prose, however, is a deep compassion for the human condition. The Hemingway style is much tougher than the message conveyed by it.

It is this spare language and this tough attitude that have been widely imitated, sometimes to the point of parody. Little Caesar (W. R. Burnett's gangster) and Sam Spade (Dashiell Hammett's private detective) are Hemingway's illegitimate offspring.

In Hemingway's best work, especially in the successful short stories, the taut, uncluttered language forces the reader to supply the emotional concomitant. Hemingway was completely aware of what he was doing. In *Death in the Afternoon* he explains his method:

> If a writer of prose knows enough about what he is writing about he may omit things that he knows and the reader, if the writer is writing truly enough, will have a feeling of those things as strongly as though the writer had stated them. The dignity of movement of an iceberg is due to only one-eighth of it being above water.

It has been said repeatedly that Hemingway's style is his greatest achievement. If achievement is measured mainly by influence on other writers, that judgment is correct. The stature of a writer in the long run, however, is determined in equal measure by what he said about his own time, and by its continuing applicability to all time. In short, the critical emphasis on Hemingway as stylist does not do justice to him. He has not been given credit for bringing to fiction a new dimension, some new correspondence with the indefinable *reality* that creative literature strives to fathom. In some way he has brought literature closer to life. If he offers no apocalyptic vision, he still leaves us with the feeling that this is the way things really are.

2

○○

Oak Park
to Paris

In the year of Ernest Hemingway's birth, 1899, his parents contracted for the building of a summer cottage on the shores of Walloon Lake (at that time called Bear Lake) near the town of Petoskey in northern Michigan. The lake and environs became the backdrop for many of his short stories. This is the land of the fictional Big Two-Hearted River where Nick Adams first experienced the joy and sadness of life and where he was initiated into the realities of love, violence, and death. The boy Hemingway passed his summers at Walloon Lake—camping, fishing, hunting—and there he developed the attachment to the outdoors that was to remain a lifelong passion.

Hemingway's father was Dr. Clarence Edmonds Hemingway, usually called Ed, a general practitioner of medicine. His mother, Grace Hall Hemingway, met her future husband while they were students at the high school in Oak Park, a suburban town near Chicago. There Ernest was born, the Hemingways' first son and second child; ultimately the family would consist of six children, four girls and two boys.

Ed Hemingway was a tall, powerful man with whom Ernest was able to identify easily and from whom he learned to love nature. Cookery—he loved all kinds of fish and game—was one of Ed's special skills. He was an enthusiastic collector of archeological artifacts and animal specimens. Gifted with extraordinary eyesight and a fine shot with a rifle, he taught Ernest the arts of shooting, fishing, and camping. The boy sometimes accompanied his father on emergency medical calls around Petoskey. Nick Adams, the hero of some of Hemingway's early stories, accompanies his father, also a doctor, on such calls.

Nick's close attachment to his father parallels Hemingway's relationship with Ed. The growing boy finds in the father, in both fiction and life, not only a teacher-guide but a fixed refuge against the terrors of the emotional and spiritual unknown as they are encountered. In his father Ernest had someone to lean on.

There was also the inevitable revolt from the authority figure. Ed Hemingway was a harsh disciplinarian in the puritan mold. His lectures to the boy extolled purity of body and mind. He conjured up hellfire to warn the boy against giving in to the temptations of the flesh. Sometimes the boy hated his father, although the underlying relationship between them was warm and affectionate. Carlos Baker, in his richly detailed biography, *Ernest Hemingway: A Life Story*, tells us that "Ernest reported that when his father had punished him and he was angry, he had sometimes sat in the open door of the shed with his shotgun, drawing a bead on his father's head."

In some of his stories Hemingway idealized Ed, as adults often idealize the fathers of their youth: for the adult Ernest his father's eyesight became more keen, his muscles more powerful. The manner of his father's death, however, was a painful subject for Hemingway. In 1928, Ed Hemingway, ill and depressed, and unable to sleep, committed suicide by shooting himself with his father's old Civil War revolver. The adult Ernest, for whom death was an obsession and who often speculated on suicide, returned repeatedly in his fiction to the suicide of fathers. Nick Adams's father kills himself, as does Robert Jordan's in *For Whom the Bell Tolls*. Hemingway always feared losing his physical and mental powers in old age. Like his father, he ended his life by shooting himself during a period of severe depression.

The psychological questions raised by the relationship between Ernest and his father call for further inves-

tigation. The mature Hemingway always had a need
for self-assertion and mastery. He cast himself in the
role of an authoritarian father figure, even to his relish
for the "Papa" designation that he carried for most of
his adult life. He never forgave his mother for bully-
ing his father, nor his father for allowing her to do it.

Hemingway resented anyone, even close friends,
who seemed to be assuming a proprietary role toward
him. Sudden angry flareups, often without substantial
basis, were not uncommon. These unpredictable out-
bursts lost him many friends of long standing. Despite
his mercurial temperament, however, friends in need of
assistance found him kind and generous. On one side,
observers noted that Hemingway needed to be the im-
movable figure, the tower of strength, the patriarch
who stood alone. Yet many people of excellent judgment found him to be shy, overly sensitive, and unsure
of himself in speech and act. Both observations are true.
Hemingway was not a simple man. Perhaps he was un-
consciously defending the image of Ed Hemingway.

Although Ernest's boyhood was externally normal
and happy, the Hemingway household was not peace-
ful. Ed and Grace quarreled, usually about money and
the raising of the children. Grace, a frustrated opera
singer, was an avid seeker of culture in the chautauqua
manner; she spiritualized everything. She reflected the
gentility of much nineteenth-century middle-class culture, born of the New England tradition but drained of
its original vitality. Ed's scientific interests and his attachment to the outdoor life saved him from the worst
aspects of this watery culture. The adolescent Ernest
increasingly lost sympathy for his mother. The relationship degenerated further as the years passed, becoming worse after his father's suicide. It is perhaps
significant that the ideal Hemingway heroine was the

opposite of the aggressive female. She was loving, tender, submissive, and served the needs of her man. Hemingway heroines have no housework problems, no career problems. Like Freud and D. H. Lawrence, Hemingway believed in male supremacy.

Hemingway received his formal education in the public schools of Oak Park. In high school he was an excellent English student and generally satisfactory in the other subjects. He worked as a reporter on the school newspaper, his first contact with the journalism that was to be his entrée into the world beyond Oak Park. He had begun to write stories while he was in junior high school, usually with himself as hero in difficult situations. He continued writing stories for the high school literary magazine, modeling them after Ring Lardner, who was then a well-known sports columnist with the Chicago *Tribune*, and after Jack London's violent tales of primitive life. It was while he was still in high school that he began to consider a career in journalism and fiction.

Hemingway was deeply interested in all sports, an interest that remained with him throughout his life. He made the football team at Oak Park as a second-string lineman. Tall for his age but clumsy with adolescence and without the weight and muscle of the adult man, he was not outstanding in team sports. His preferences were always for camping, canoeing, swimming, fishing, and shooting. When he was sixteen he took up boxing, discovered that he had a talent for it, and with the passage of time developed into a skilled amateur boxer. He was not above acting the bully when he had a pair of boxing gloves on his hands. In later years Hemingway hinted that he had been tutored by professional boxers in Chicago gyms, an improbable story.

The family had half-expected him to follow his

father into medicine. On graduation from high school in June 1917, however, he rejected college. Through the efforts of his Uncle Tyler, Hemingway landed a job as cub reporter on the Kansas City *Star*. There was some talk of joining the army (in the spring the United States had declared war on Germany), but Ed was opposed to it because of Ernest's youth, and Ernest did not press the issue.

He was anxious to get away from the overseeing eyes of his parents and to strike out on his own. Kansas City was rough and bustling, with more than its share of violence, crime, and prostitution. The young reporter's assignments in the hospitals and courts introduced him to the underside of American urban life. Directly, the experience was of use to Hemingway in several of his early sketches; indirectly, it contributed to the development of a tough sophistication that worked against moral clichés and genteel preaching.

Perhaps the most important positive effect of the Kansas City *Star* interlude was its influence on Hemingway's style. He was being trained as a newspaper writer. The journalistic virtues—objectivity, terseness, clarity—were enshrined in the *Star* stylebook and were emphasized in advice from older colleagues. Hemingway learned to value the short, simple declarative sentence, to avoid the descriptive and therefore often subjective adjective. If the nouns and verbs are accurate the reader will find the appropriate emotional response.

Above all, newspaper writing must be readable. Popular journalism had exerted a strong influence on American prose after the Civil War. The newspaper addressed itself to the growing literate population, most of whom Harvard prose could not attract. Mark Twain and Stephen Crane, both coming to fiction from a newspaper background, were among the few direct literary influences on Hemingway. Their prose style, close to the pattern of the everyday spoken language, pointed toward Hemingway and away from the more ornate academic style of the New England tradition.

Hemingway, having applied to the American Red Cross for service as an ambulance driver, resigned from the *Star* in April 1918, shortly before he was called up. He took the boat for the European war theater in a spirit of high adventure and youthful enthusiasm, impatient to become part of the action. Stationed at Schio, about twenty miles from Milan in northern Italy, he found his chores as an ambulance driver not exciting enough. He volunteered for front-line canteen duty and was sent to Fossalta on the Piave River front, then the focus of a developing Austrian offensive. There Hemingway was severely wounded in an Austrian mortar and machine gun attack. He suffered multiple wounds in both legs, the severest damage being done by a machine gun slug in the right knee. Disabled as he was, he managed to carry a wounded Italian soldier to safety. For this courageous act he was awarded the Silver Medal of Valor and the Croce di Guerra and was promoted to first lieutenant in the regular Italian army.

After first-aid treatment in the field hospital he was taken to the American Red Cross Hospital in Milan, where surgery removed the bullet from his right knee and where he recuperated for a half-year, managing to take several short vacation trips with cane or on crutches. He even tried to return to his Red Cross work. In the end he was cured of his wounds and his romantic notions of war. He was not averse, however, to cutting the dashing figure in a well-tailored uniform.

In the hospital Hemingway convinced himself that he was desperately in love with an American nurse,

Agnes von Kurowsky, seven years his senior; he offered marriage. She never seems to have seriously entertained the idea of sexual consummation or marriage. Their letters to each other were affectionate in the playful romantic vein, with Agnes gradually encouraging Ernest to return to the United States according to plan while she remained in Europe. They continued a voluminous correspondence across the Atlantic until Agnes told Ernest that she had fallen in love with a young Italian officer. Ernest was temporarily prostrated with grief; he recovered. He later used the experience as the basis for a rather cynical sketch, "A Very Short Story."

Agnes was also the starting point for Hemingway's portrait of Catherine Barkley, the heroine of *A Farewell to Arms*. Hemingway's entire experience in Italy was the raw material for that novel. A Captain Serena, who was attracted to Agnes, grew into Lieutenant Rinaldi. A Count Greppi, whom Hemingway became friendly with at Lake Maggiore on one of his vacation trips from the hospital, was transformed into Count Greffi of the novel. Several of the Nick Adams stories are obviously traceable to the Italian experience. One easily recognizes Hemingway's life in his fiction, but it must be emphasized again that they are not the same.

The effects of the war experience on Hemingway the man were profound and lasted all his life. For years after Italy he left his bedroom light on at night. Insomnia plagued him. Death was always with him in dreams and nightmares.

Yet when Hemingway came home after the war he laid it on pretty thick for the people of Oak Park, with blood-curdling tales of the fighting, his own role being enlarged in the telling. His skill and courage as a boxer, hunter, and soldier became for him his indispensable credentials as a man. The legend of Hemingway the man of action was to remain with him until his death. Perhaps his need to flamboyantly assert his courage and manliness was compensation for fear and doubt, but it must be remembered that he was not merely going through a masquerade. The testimony of numerous observers is proof of his sometimes fool-hardy courage. In his adult life he insisted on plunging into dangerous situations. His courage was real, no matter how distorted his view of its significance.

If in his private life he was driven to dramatize himself as a tough guy, in his writing he drew upon all the complexities that resided in his total personality. In his best work Hemingway maintained a basic objec-tivity toward his art and toward himself that enabled him to draw on the fullness of his resources. Heming-way the artist usually transcended the narcissism of his private life. Thus in *The Sun Also Rises* and *A Fare-well to Arms*, generally considered his most successful novels, his heroes are not especially heroic. Their cen-tral quality is sensitivity to the cruelty and meaningless-ness of life. They are maimed by war, or weary, or cynical, or sick of violence and death, or frightened.

Only in some of his later fiction, notably *Across the River and Into the Trees*, did Hemingway allow his own public image as a tough guy to intrude on his art. It was a symptom of the artist in decline.

Some critics have read and judged Hemingway in the glare of his more objectionable posturing. Some make the assertion that Hemingway attracted readers by the power of his legend rather than the power of his writing. One thing is sure, the existence of the leg-end has resulted in a critical oversimplification of Hem-ingway's art and vision.

When Hemingway returned to Oak Park from Europe he was lionized by family, friends, and com-

munity. Soon, however, the home atmosphere turned
tense. Several years later Hemingway drew on this period of his life for a short story, "Soldier's Home." His
parents expected him to "settle down" into stability
and respectability. His mother felt that willingness to
help with the household chores was an index of mature
manhood. He was charged with being a freeloader.

In 1920 Ernest was offered a job in Toronto as a
companion to a crippled boy. He was left with plenty
of free time. Through the efforts of his employer, the
boy's father, he landed a job as a reporter on the Toronto *Daily Star* and as a feature writer on the weekend edition, the Toronto *Star Weekly*, which was
mainly devoted to entertaining, magazine-style articles.
Ernest wrote for the two papers for the next four
years. He was given a by-line but not much money
went with it.

He left Toronto to spend the summer of 1920 at
Walloon Lake and then returned to Oak Park. Ernest
was not comfortable in the strained situation at home;
he contrived to be away as much as possible. His parents, in a surge of righteous indignation and concern,
suggested that he depart from home to straighten himself out and to learn what it meant to be on his own.
Ernest dramatized this into an expulsion from home. In
any event, he was effectively separated from the paren-
tal ties, even though neither he nor his parents took the
separation as a hard fact. He returned to Oak Park regularly, especially for weekends when he could expect
to get good home-cooked victuals. Nevertheless, from
this time on his freedom was won; he would reach his
own decisions. He made Chicago his headquarters, living in a series of inexpensive rooms and enjoying the
active social life of a young man with plenty of friends.
In Chicago, he worked on a succession of jobs, all

vaguely connected with writing, while continuing to do articles for the *Star Weekly*.

In 1920 he met Hadley Richardson, a Saint Louis girl who had recently nursed her mother during a terminal illness. Her father had committed suicide in 1903. Hadley and Ernest fell deeply in love and planned marriage. They would go to Europe, particularly Italy, where they would see the scenes of Ernest's war adventures. They would live on the income from Hadley's small trust fund, some twenty-five hundred dollars a year. In Chicago, Hemingway had met Sherwood Anderson, at that time already famous as the author of *Winesburg, Ohio*. Anderson suggested Paris as an ideal place for a young, aspiring writer. There he would be in the company of the artistic expatriates of the Left Bank. There, in the capital of modernism, he would learn to write.

Hemingway's parents were pleased with the idea of their son's marriage. They liked Hadley and must have thought that marriage would force Ernest to overcome what they considered his irresponsibility. The newlyweds took ship for France late in 1921. Hemingway was fortified with the generous Anderson's letters of introduction to outstanding members of the expatriate colony, including Gertrude Stein and Ezra Pound. The letters recommended Hemingway as a writer of unusual promise, high praise indeed for an unpublished young fellow just turned twenty-two.

Safely but not comfortably ensconced in an inexpensive flat, the Hemingways set out to explore Paris and to make contact with the expatriate group. Ernest loved Paris. He met Sylvia Beach, the owner of the famous Shakespeare and Company bookstore who became a good friend and could be counted on for a loan in time of need. He began what turned out to be a rather stormy personal and literary acquaintanceship with Ford Madox Ford. He met and occasionally talked with James Joyce, one of his major literary heroes. After the publication of Hemingway's small first volume, *Three Stories and Ten Poems*, Scott Fitzgerald sought him out. They developed a friendship that lasted through periodic clashes and misunderstandings.

Pound, always ready to help young writers, immediately took Hemingway under his wing. He pontificated at length for the enlightenment of the young man and offered to teach him how to write if the young man would teach him how to box. It was a deal that worked out better for Hemingway than for Pound, who had no talent for pugilism. Later in life, however, Hemingway said that Pound's literary advice had always seemed good when given but had usually turned out to be wide of the mark.

Gertrude Stein, officiating from her Paris "salon" apartment, was the high priestess of the expatriate circle and the arbiter of literary modernism. It was considered a necessity for young writers to seek her advice and possibly her approbation. Hemingway called on her and read aloud some of his poems, and parts of a novel that he had given up on. She liked the poems more than the prose. The young man seemed to be deeply interested in her observations, a quality that Gertrude Stein valued above all others. Ernest became, or she thought he became, her protégé. Now the one thing Hemingway was constitutionally incapable of being was a protégé. He was not the man to worship at another's shrine.

For several years his relationship with Miss Stein was harmonious—she was godmother to his first son—but after the publication of *The Sun Also Rises* the friendship cooled when she began to hint that she was responsible for Hemingway's success. He resented the notion that he was a student in anyone's school. In her memoirs, *The Autobiography of Alice B. Toklas*, published in 1933, she charged that Hemingway was a coward and a braggart. In *A Moveable Feast*, published posthumously, Hemingway retorted that she had learned more about writing from him than he from her, and that it was his influence that had eased the way for publication of her writings. In fairness to Hemingway it should be noted that Gertrude Stein quarreled at one time or another with almost all her associates.

Years later, when Hemingway looked back on his relationship with Gertrude Stein, he conceded that her suggestions for the improvement of his writing were usually justified and useful. Her linguistic theories, occasionally cloudy to the point of unintelligibility, ran parallel in some particulars to Hemingway's own line of development. Her *Three Lives*, especially the novella "Melanctha," was written in a simple, uncluttered prose style that at least superficially resembles Hemingway's. He agreed with her belief that fiction should convey a feeling of factual and emotional immediacy, a sense of the actual present.

Hemingway was repeatedly involved in literary wars; the pattern came to be familiar and lasted throughout his life. For one thing, he was too ready to attack the shortcomings of his literary friends. He offered for publication in a magazine that Pound was foreign editor of, a satire attacking Pound's romantic bohemianism. Fortunately it was not published. Hemingway did not like the bohemian life style. Although in time he developed his own share of affectations, he reacted against the arty and theatrical in the expatriate community.

Another source of personal squabbles was Hemingway's use of recognizable people in his fiction. They were not always flattered by the portraits.

In Paris Hemingway worked hard to become a writer. He continued to experiment with poetry, which he still believed was his true calling, but he increasingly worked on stories. He read carefully the great fiction writers—Balzac, Flaubert, Tolstoy, Dostoyevsky, Turgenev, Twain, Crane, James, Conrad, and Joyce. Largely self-educated, Hemingway remained an omnivorous reader all his life. Unsympathetic to the academic mentality, he was nevertheless well informed on the literary, social, and political issues of his time.

Departing from the pattern of his juvenilia, Hemingway's earliest published stories turned away from overt representation of violence. It was still there but usually as an undercurrent. The plots were not rounded out after the classic Aristotelean formula. The unity of the stories depended more on the achievement of an emotional tone in the Anderson manner (Hemingway admitted that his first important models were the stories in *Winesburg, Ohio.*) The rejection letters from American editors complained that Hemingway's stories were not really stories at all.

He also worked on short, impressionistic prose sketches, compressed rigorously to catch the event at the precise moment when emotional essentials were revealed. He worked hard on the basic tools of his art: how to be true to the cadence of the spoken language, how to say more in fewer words, how to convey the desired emotion without directly telling the reader what he was supposed to feel. It is clear that Hemingway was then and remained all his life a serious, committed artist.

Hemingway's assignments for the Toronto *Daily Star* and *Star Weekly* gave him an opportunity to travel extensively. He covered the major political and military stories of the early 1920s in France, Switzerland, Italy, and the Black Sea area. With Hadley he managed to take fishing, skiing, and sightseeing vacations. A tour of Spain with some friends stirred his lifelong enthusiasm for bullfighting.

Hadley was pregnant, and the Hemingways decided to return to Canada so that the child could be born on American soil. In 1923, just before they sailed, Hemingway's first volume of writings was published in a small Paris edition. *Three Stories and Ten Poems* was a thin volume, but there it was, something tangible. Hemingway was in high spirits. The child, a son, was born in Canada, and as soon as he was old enough to travel, the Hemingways sailed for Paris. While they were still in Canada, the short sketches that Hemingway had written in Paris were published, again in a small Paris edition, under the title *in our time*. In 1925, with the help of Donald Ogden Stewart, who had been a member of the expatriate group in Paris, the three stories of *Three Stories and Ten Poems* and the sketches of *in our time*, supplemented by a larger group of new stories, were published in America by Boni and Liveright under the title *In Our Time*.

The stories that comprised *In Our Time* were each introduced by one of the sketches from the Paris *in our time*. Some critics profess to see a loose thematic connection in the pairings.

One of the sketches introduces Nick Adams in an Italian war scene:

Nick sat against the wall of the church where they had dragged him to be clear of machine-gun fire in the street. Both legs stuck out awkwardly. He had been hit in the spine. His face was sweaty and dirty. The sun shone on his face. The day was very hot. Rinaldi, big backed, his equip-

ment sprawling, lay face downward against the wall. Nick
looked straight ahead brilliantly. The pink wall of the
house opposite had fallen out from the roof, and an iron
bedstead hung twisted toward the street. Two Austrian
dead lay in the rubble in the shade of the house. Up the
street were other dead. Things were getting forward in the
town. It was going well. Stretcher bearers would be along
any time now. Nick turned his head and looked down at
Rinaldi. "Senta Rinaldi; Senta. You and me we've made a
separate peace." Rinaldi lay still in the sun, breathing with
difficulty. "We're not patriots." Nick turned his head away,
smiling sweatily. Rinaldi was a disappointing audience.

This is the entire sketch, obviously based on Hemingway's own experience on the Piave. The most significant feature is the emergence of the Hemingway
style. The experimental writing in Paris had eventu-
ated in an economical, honed literary instrument. The
sentences are short and declarative, with just enough
variation to avert monotony. Longer sentences are composed of the same short units joined by the noncom-
mittal *and*. Hemingway rarely used the subordinating
conjunctions like *since* and *although* that enable a
writer to do the thinking and feeling for the reader.
Hemingway induces the emotion; he does not describe
it. The reader must make the logical connections and
capture the emotional tone without the aid of direc-
tional signals. Hemingway's is an art that insists on the
re-creation of the emotion by the reader himself.

Instead of describing the general destruction in the
town, Hemingway picks out small segments that he
treats with pinpoint accuracy: "The pink wall of the
house opposite had fallen out from the roof, and an
iron bedstead hung twisted toward the street." The art
of omission is effective only when what is included is
the essential. This is a style that is deceptively simple

but that requires painstaking artistic conscience. It is a style that does not show the sweat that goes into it.

The short stories were well received by the more perceptive critics, among whom were Edmund Wilson, Paul Rosenfeld, and Allen Tate. The consensus was that a fresh, original talent had appeared on the literary scene.

"Indian Camp" deals with an incident in the boyhood of Nick Adams. His father, a physician, has been called to attend an Indian woman who is in serious difficulty giving birth to her child. Nick and his Uncle George accompany Dr. Adams in the middle of the night as he is rowed across a lake to the Indian village. The doctor decides that only an immediate caesarean section can save the woman and child. He prepares to operate by lamplight in the Indian shanty, using a jack-knife as scalpel. There is no anesthetic and the woman screams horribly throughout the operation. The baby is born, the mother's wound sewed up with a gut fishing leader. During the operation, the woman's husband lay quietly in the upper bunk, his head covered by a blanket to muffle the screams of his wife. When Dr. Adams finally turns to check the husband it is discovered that he is dead. Unable to bear her screams, he had killed himself by cutting his throat from ear to ear.

The suicide of the Indian seems to be a gratuitous turn. In the context of the situation as given, it is too extreme an action. The psychological basis for the suicide is thin; the Indian is not even described. A reader may justifiably feel that the incident was inserted for its shock effect, a gruesome O. Henry twist. The violence, however, is not the heart of the story. In the eight short pages of the story we see how Nick Adams, perhaps every boy, one day must come face to face with pain, birth, and death, and must begin to look for

answers that are never to be discovered. Hidden behind Hemingway's laconic style and surface objectivity
is a most sensitive evocation of the human predicament.

In "Indian Camp" we do not know Nick's exact
age, but it becomes clear that he is a rather young boy,
perhaps ten. While the Indians row two boats across
the lake to the woman, Nick and his father sit in the
stern of one boat. "Nick lay back with his father's arm
around him." In the shanty the father explains to Nick
in simple medical terms why the woman is screaming.
Nick asks: "Oh, Daddy, can't you give her something
to make her stop screaming?" Hemingway makes no
attempt to take the reader into Nick's mind; all we
have is the bare question to which Dr. Adams must answer that there is no anesthetic.

After the baby is born, Dr. Adams goes on with
his scientific explanation. He tells Nick that the inci-
sion must be closed. At this juncture, Hemingway tells
us that "Nick did not watch. His curiosity has been
gone for a long time." We are never told directly why
Nick was no longer curious about the progress of the
operation. The reader must see that Nick had that
night already come into contact with enough of the
harshness of life to shock him into revulsion and fear.

Later, when the bloody corpse of the husband is
discovered, Dr. Adams tells Uncle George to "take
Nick out of the shanty," but it is too late. Nick had
seen everything when his father had held up a lamp to
examine the Indian.

Dr. Adams expresses regret for having brought
Nick with him and having thereby subjected him to a
disturbing experience. Nick, in response, overflows
with the questions that are troubling him:

"Do ladies always have such a hard time having ba-
bies?" Nick asked.

"No, that was very, very exceptional."

"Why did he kill himself, Daddy?"

"I don't know, Nick. He couldn't stand things, I guess."

"Do many men kill themselves, Daddy?"

"Not very many, Nick."

"Do many women?"

"Hardly ever."

"Don't they ever?"

"Oh, yes. They do sometimes."

"Daddy?"

"Yes."

"Where did Uncle George go?"

"He'll turn up all right."

"Is dying hard, Daddy?"

"No, I think it's pretty easy, Nick. It all depends.

Returning from the Indian village, Dr. Adams rows, with Nick seated alone in the stern of the boat. The dawn is up, and Nick is returning to life from the darkness of the experience in the Indian shanty:

A bass jumped, making a circle in the water. Nick trailed his hand in the water. It felt warm in the sharp chill of the morning.

In the early morning on the lake sitting in the stern of the boat with his father rowing, he felt quite sure that he would never die.

There is irony in Nick's conviction that he would never die. The reader suspects at the end that it is based on the boy's wish for belief rather than a confident belief in the sheltering strength of his father. Although technically the omniscient author is telling the story, he unobtrusively becomes one with Nick. The shadowy Nick, who is, in effect, telling his own story, however, must be an older Nick who is looking back nostalgically on his own youthful capacity for faith even though the events of the story show us a loss of innocence. The irony acquires an additional dimension through the older Nick's implicit awareness of the original irony in the young Nick's experience.

Hemingway in these early stories establishes the central design of his writing. He is not so much the analyst of violence as of the sensitive man in a world that does not make sense. His imitators picked up the violence and toughness, and the tight-lipped style. They vulgarized the Hemingway vision, which depends on the tension between a tough prose in a tough world and compassion for men with their dreams of a lost Eden. An essentially tragic pattern in modern terms, though assuredly not the heroic mood of Shakespearean tragedy, emerges. When Hemingway fails the tension relaxes into mock heroics or sentimentality. In his best work, the tension holds firmly.

Most of the stories of *In Our Time* are not concerned with violence at all. The integrating element is a deep interest in the nuances of human relationships: husband and wife, father and son, young man and his girl friend, friend and friend. In "Cat in the Rain" and "Out of Season" Hemingway captures a most elusive mental and emotional atmosphere in the lives of a young husband and wife. Through low-keyed attention to things and facts Hemingway evokes the desired emotional tones.

"Big Two-Hearted River" is the longest story of *In Our Time*. For sheer descriptive power it is a masterpiece. The plot line is simple to the point of not seeming to be there at all. A grown-up Nick Adams is the only character. He walks from town to the river; he sets up camp in the pines along the riverbank. He eats and goes to sleep. The next day he fishes the stream and nets a couple of good ones. That is all.

For a long time the strength of this well-regarded story was considered to be its masterful evocation of nature. The evaluation is sound as far as it goes, but there is much more to see and say.

In Part I Nick, having alighted from the train on which he had been a passenger, gazes at the burned-out town of Seney. He finds it difficult to recognize the place, since the familiar buildings and other landmarks are gone. Only the river is still there to reassure him. He walks out of the town into the open country, passing fields and hillsides blackened by the fire. He breaks out into rolling green pine country and heads for the river. He finds a suitable place near the shore, spreads blankets for a bed, and pitches his tent over the blankets. He makes a fire and warms canned beans and spaghetti, which he eats with good appetite. With water drawn from the river he prepares a pot of coffee. He opens a can of apricots for dessert and drinks his coffee. He goes to sleep in the tent.

In Part II, Nick rises early, goes to catch grasshoppers for bait and stores them in a bottle. Then he breakfasts on buckwheat cakes and coffee. He cuts bread for two onion sandwiches, which he makes and packs away in his knapsack for lunch. Then he fishes the river, bracing himself against the swift current. He catches an undersized trout and returns it to freedom. He hooks an immense trout whose struggles snap the line. Finally, he lands two good trout, guts and cleans them, and heads back to camp.

As in "Indian Camp," careful reading reveals further dimensions in "Big Two-Hearted River." When Nick leaves the burned-out town he walks across the bridge over the river and sees the trout in the water below. We learn that "it was a long time since Nick had looked into a stream and seen trout." Hemingway never tells us directly the reasons for Nick's long absence from the Big Two-Hearted River, nor is it necessary for appreciation of the story. It is enough if the reader sees that something has kept Nick away. A regular reader of Hemingway might know from other stories (most of them written later) that Nick had gone to war and had been wounded in Italy, recovering in body after many months, and in mind not even now. On the bridge "Nick's heart tightened as the trout moved. He felt all the old feeling." It becomes clear that Nick is trying to recapture an old relationship with the Big Two-Hearted River. He walks on:

It was hard work walking up-hill. His muscles ached and the day was hot but Nick felt happy. He felt he had left every thing behind, the need for thinking, the need to write, other things. It was all back of him.

Whatever Nick was leaving behind, it had been painful. Thinking was painful; writing was painful. In the reference to writing, Nick fades into Hemingway himself.

Nick has come back to the river to find his life again, in a sense to be reborn in the waters. Thus far it is working out:

From the time he had gotten off the train and the baggage man had thrown his pack out of the open car door things had been different. Seney was burned, the country was burned over and changed but it did not matter. It could not all be burned. He knew that.

Nick is recovering his spiritual balance. He has passed through the fire—the war, Seney—but the world is still the world. The river, the pines, the fish, all say that the earth endures forever. Yet a doubt lingers in Nick's mind. "He knew that" has a desperate undertone; he is trying hard to convince himself that all is well.

He pitches his tent and crawls in:

Inside the tent the light came through the brown canvas. It smelled pleasantly of canvas. Already there was something mysterious and homelike. Nick was happy as he crawled inside the tent. He had not been unhappy all day. This was different though. Now things were done. It had been a hard trip. He was very tired. That was done. He had made his camp. He was settled. Nothing could touch him. It was a good place to camp. He was there, in the good place. He was in his home where he had made it. Now he was hungry.

Nick continues to make connections. He notes that he had not been unhappy all day, as though that were unusual. In Nick's general condition, unhappiness must have been the rule. Now, however, he has gone beyond the negative virtue of not having been unhappy. Because he was doing things, fending for himself, a positive quality has entered his life. He sounds a note of contentment, tentative and defensive though it be. Nick is throwing off his disease. When he warms the beans and spaghetti he convinces himself that he does not have to apologize to the universe: "I've got a right to eat this kind of stuff, if I'm willing to carry it." Nick is asserting his wholeness and his right to life in this setting that accepts him.

From the sunny part of the river where Nick fishes, he can see the swamp through which the narrowing river flows. It is a dark place overhung with low branches of cedar. A man would be compelled to bend "almost level with the ground" to walk through that swamp. Nick decides not to fish the swamp: "In the fast, deep water, in the half light, the fishing would be tragic. In the swamp fishing was a tragic adventure.

Nick did not want it." In the end, as Nick prepares to
return to camp with his catch, he thinks "there were
plenty of days coming when he could fish the swamp,"
that is, when he would be strong enough to face the
shadows.

Much can be made of the symbols in the story.
The burned-out land through which Nick passes is the
dark world in which he has been living. The swamp
remains as the dark reminder of that world. Hemingway's symbols, however, are never an easy out for a
failure to come to grips with the raw experience itself.
The symbolic values in Hemingway's art do not enter
into the reader's consciousness as symbols at all. Hemingway achieves a broadening and universality of
meaning by relying on situations and objects that will
from within develop the wider implications. The
method is closer to that found in writers before symbolism became a self-conscious literary movement.
There are symbols in Hemingway but he is no sym-
bolist.

3

The Lost
Generation

When measured by the number of copies sold, *In Our Time* was not a great success; Hemingway was still virtually unknown to the American reading public. He had, however, been brought to the attention of the important critics and had won the high regard of some of the outstanding creative writers of the time. Scott Fitzgerald persistently praised Hemingway as "the real thing" on the contemporary literary scene. He recommended Hemingway to Scribner's. Maxwell Perkins, Fitzgerald's editor at Scribner's and a most perceptive judge of literary talent, began a correspondence with Hemingway, who promised to give Scribner's first crack at his writings if the arrangements with Boni and Liveright did not work out.

Late in 1925 Hemingway had completed the first draft of a novel, *The Sun Also Rises*, dealing with life among the Left Bank expatriates. Before starting the final revision he relaxed by turning out a satiric novel, *The Torrents of Spring*, which ridiculed the fuzzier aspects of Sherwood Anderson's work. The "torrents" are the vague longings for "real life" that swirl around Yogi Johnson, a war veteran, and Scripps Howard, a foot-loose literary man. In the end, the torrents bring Scripps his true love, and sweep the naked Yogi back to the woods accompanied by an equally clothesless Indian squaw.

Against the advice of John Dos Passos and Hadley, Hemingway decided to go through with the publication of *The Torrents of Spring*. Anderson's sentimentality and extravagant primitivism, particularly in *Dark Laughter*, were the central targets of the parody, with Gertrude Stein and others being subjected to lesser punishment. The attack, though justifiable from the literary point of view, seemed in bad taste coming from Hemingway, whom Anderson had befriended and helped. Hemingway may have seen in his book an opportunity to declare his literary independence. Reviewers of *In Our Time* had pointed out, to Hemingway's annoyance, substantial Andersonian primitivism in the stories; some had remarked on the similarity between "My Old Man" and Anderson's racetrack stories. The reviewers were wrong; Hemingway was not a primitive, and what was most significant in the stories was not the result of Anderson's influence. Hemingway might have left the situation to right itself with the passage of time, but his fierce need for independence won out. Not unexpectedly the victims struck back, Gertrude Stein with vituperation, Anderson more mildly.

Hemingway sent *The Torrents of Spring* to Boni and Liveright, who turned it down, as might have been expected. After all, Anderson was their leading writer; they could hardly publish a satire ridiculing him. Their rejection of the book enabled Hemingway to break his contract with Liveright and switch to Scribner's as his publisher. Hemingway later insisted that this eventuality had not entered his mind when he wrote the book. Nevertheless, Scribner's represented a step up. When rejecting *The Torrents of Spring*, Boni and Liveright made it clear that they wanted to publish *The Sun Also Rises*, but the original contract with Hemingway was drawn in such terms that Hemingway was within his legal rights in changing publishers. Scribner's published *The Torrents of Spring* in 1926.

It was at this time that Hemingway's marriage broke down. By mutual consent Hadley and Ernest set up separate households; the divorce followed in 1927. Ernest had fallen in love with Pauline Pfeiffer, a wealthy girl from Arkansas whom he had met in Paris.

Hemingway was not happy about the turn in his domestic life; his marriage with Hadley had seemed to be a success. He blamed himself for its collapse. He went through a period of emotional turmoil during which the idea of suicide kept revolving in his mind, as it did from time to time through his entire life. It is impossible to estimate the seriousness of these ruminations. In any event, soon after his divorce was final, Pauline Pfeiffer became his second wife.

In 1926 Scribner's brought out *The Sun Also Rises*, which established Hemingway as a major literary figure and which is considered by many critics to be his best novel. It deals with the lives of a group of American and English expatriates in Paris after World War I. In an atmosphere of weary disillusionment obscured by a frenetic gaiety, they make the rounds of the bistros, drink too much, play the sex game without conviction, and through it all, make jokes about the wounds that the war has inflicted on their bodies and souls. The central figure and narrator is Jake Barnes, a correspondent for an American press service. He has been emasculated by a war wound and is thus without hope in his love for Lady Brett Ashley. Brett, deeply in love with Jake and engaged to marry the hard-drinking Mike Campbell, is involved in both casual and serious love affairs while awaiting a divorce from her husband. Robert Cohn, the son of a wealthy New York Jewish family, is another of the group. He falls in love with Brett, who spends a weekend with him in Spain before deciding to break off the affair. The group also includes Bill Gorton, a successful writer and close friend of Jake Barnes.

All meet at Pamplona in northern Spain to enjoy the fiesta. Cohn cannot believe that Brett is through with him; he follows her tenaciously. Mike, usually drunk, repeatedly insults Cohn in the hope that he can be pressured into leaving. When Brett falls in love with

Pedro Romero, a young torero, the tension between Cohn and the others is aggravated. A fist fight ensues in which Cohn, a skilled boxer, knocks down Mike and Jake. Cohn goes to Romero's room and gives him a severe beating in the presence of Brett. Unable to break Romero's spirit, Cohn returns to his own room where he breaks down in tears. The party is over. Brett goes off to Madrid with Romero, who offers marriage, but she decides that she is not good for him and gives him up. In the end she returns to Jake and Mike in Paris; the pattern has not changed.

As soon as the novel was published the guessing game began. Most of the characters were said to be recognizably derived from specific members of the expatriate set. Hemingway's friends believed they had been traduced in the novel. Brett was drawn from the very much emancipated Lady Duff Twysden. Harold Loeb, assumed to be the original for Cohn, later defended himself by telling the story of what "actually" happened at the festival in Pamplona. With equal irrelevancy Hemingway answered that Loeb's version was how Loeb would like it to have been. That Hemingway had worked very close to his lived experience is clear, but he had not written a stenographic report.

Literary gossip had it that Jake Barnes was a self-pitying portrait of Hemingway himself. He was roasted in the Freudian coals: he was said to have a castration complex, or repressed sexual fear, or latent homosexuality. *The Sun Also Rises* enjoyed an initial success as a scandalous *roman à clef*. When the storm passed, the novel remained and grew in esteem on its own solid merits until it was accepted as one of the classic American novels.

A side effect of the novel was its influence on American life, particularly on Ivy League undergraduates. The 1920s was the era of postwar prosperity in America, the big boom before the big bust of 1929. Prohibition had put the speakeasy into business. Nineteenth-century moral standards were dissolving in a flood of bootleg liquor. The antics of Brett and her playmates were glamorous in the eyes of American youth. The blunt, laconic speech of the Hemingway characters became a badge of sophistication; the tour of the barrooms became a proof of emancipation. The way of life that Hemingway subjected to dispassionate analysis in his book was imitated enthusiastically by young Americans. The phenomenon is not unusual in literary history. Goethe's *The Sorrows of Young Werther*, offering as its central character a young man overwhelmed by passion, set the fashion for a whole generation of romantic nympholepts. Dostoyevsky's Raskolnikov, in *Crime and Punishment*, spawned an army of would-be supermen.

In his portrayal of the expatriates Hemingway himself was not free from emotional ambiguity. Their way of life gives them a freedom that is not without attractions for an age bent on breaking the fetters of puritanism. In his personal life Hemingway liked the sophisticated barroom atmosphere without making it a central issue in human experience. It would be a serious misreading of Hemingway to conclude that he is an advocate for Brett Ashley's way of life, but it would be equally erroneous to deny the attractiveness of the expatriates' honesty with themselves, or their stoic endurance, or their capacity for camaraderie.

Just as Fitzgerald's *This Side of Paradise* was tagged with the catch phrase "jazz age," so *The Sun Also Rises* came to be associated with "the lost generation." In Fitzgerald's case, the tag does not convey the whole truth; in Hemingway's, it conveys little of the truth.

The epigraphs that introduce *The Sun Also Rises* were misinterpreted so that Hemingway came out as a sympathetic observer of the disillusioned postwar generation. The two epigraphs were taken as reinforcement of each other when they were actually counterposed. The first epigraph is from Gertrude Stein: "You are all a lost generation." She was repeating the remark, oracularly broadening its application, of a French garage owner who complained to her about the lack of skill of his young mechanics. Hemingway certainly never regarded himself as lost or his generation as lost. In fact he objected to the presumption that any generation could be characterized in a phrase. Hemingway himself was aggressively un-lost.

The second epigraph is a quotation from the biblical Ecclesiastes: "One generation passeth away, and another generation cometh; but the earth abideth forever. . . ." Hemingway was taken aback when readers concluded that the pessimistic philosophy of Ecclesiastes and the specific reference to the generations in his epigraph were intended to strengthen the observation from Gertrude Stein. In *The Sun Also Rises* the earth— the Spanish earth, nature anywhere—is presented as an alternative to the feverish life of the expatriates. Hemingway never quite decided, however, that nature of itself offered a total alternative, that is, a complete way of life in the twentieth century.

When Jake goes fishing with Bill in the Irati River near Burguete, it is a return to Nick's Big Two-Hearted River. The cold mountain stream flows from northern Michigan to Spain or any other land where Hemingway goes. Wherever he wanders he takes with him something of Henry Thoreau and the mountain men of the Rockies. This is not, however, a cult of the primitive; Hemingway did not advocate a return to nature as a final solution for modern man. It is difficult to imagine Hemingway remaining at Walden Pond or the Irati River for more than a few days before returning to the city. For one thing he felt that one should never engage in any one activity for too long a period or boredom would destroy the pleasure.

Hemingway did not allow his feeling for nature to become cultish or quirky; he never forgot that he was a twentieth-century man. He would probably have laughed at the contemporary rural commune movement. Nature, for Hemingway, represents truth and avoidance of the pretentious. The good and the beautiful have something to do with the natural, the unspoiled. Whatever is put-on, showy, inflated in any way, is to be opposed. Although one is most likely to find the unspoiled in nature and in simple peasants, it may be discovered in the midst of urban corruption in men who refuse to accept that corruption even though they must live with it, sometimes even use it.

The young bullfighter, Romero, making his living in a corrupt business, holds to an unadorned purity of style in the bullring. He faces danger—that is how life must be for any man—he works close to the bulls, but he eschews tricks and artificialities that make the encounter *seem* more dangerous than it is. Romero stands by the truth. The Spanish peasants stand by the truth; they live without playing the roles assigned by a technological society using advertising techniques. Jake Barnes, with all his bitter knowledge and experience, also stands by the truth.

At its worst, Hemingway's scorn for the fake and the phony became itself an affectation, especially in his later fiction. It became on occasion a style divorced from substantial content, a posture rather than a serious view of life. At its best, it gives Hemingway's art a solid grip on the real, on what actually is, and makes him an important analyst of the spiritual ills of our time.

Robert Cohn suffers from illusions; he does not really know himself or his world. He plays at writing novels and hangs around the fringes of the expatriate set. Never fully accepted into the charmed circle, he is both naive and weak. He fails to stand by the truth not because he is dishonest but because he lives in a make-believe world. He falls for Brett at first sight. They go away together for a few days, after which she has had enough of him. Cohn cannot bring himself to accept the fact that Brett is not in love with him. Otherwise, he reasons, she would not have gone away with him. At Pamplona he casts himself in the impossible role of knight-defender of his lady's honor. He even convinces himself that she will not marry Mike since she does not love him. Cohn is receptive to all sorts of romantic illusions. Before he falls in love with Brett he presses Jake to take a trip with him to South America, where life is bound to be exciting. It seems that he had read W. H. Hudson's *The Purple Land* and had been much taken with South America's possibilities for genteel military adventure and high-minded love.

Cohn is the eternal dependent, a hollow man who lacks the inner strength to enter upon any relationship without being dissolved in the process. Characteristically his tennis game goes to pieces when he falls in love with Brett. D. H. Lawrence, through the figure of Gerald Crich in *Women in Love*, dealt with the same problem of a man who, seemingly self-assured, lacks a firm identity from within. Hemingway returned to the theme with Francis Macomber (in "The Short Happy

Life of Francis Macomber"), who cannot bring himself
to leave his bitch of a wife because she is beautiful and
he is not sure that he can do better.

The quality of maleness, the archetypal pride of
the male, is an important consideration in Hemingway.
The male does not crawl to the female. Love is not a
refuge from personality or a leap into oblivion. What
Hemingway has in mind is more than physical; it includes a spiritual, mythic element. The stress on mas-
culinity may degenerate, as indeed it does in some of
Hemingway's later work, into mere glorification of the
hairy chest. In the contemporary Women's Liberation
context it leaves Hemingway open to the charge of
male chauvinism, since his ideal women are mainly interested in serving their men's needs. From a broadly
social point of view, however, Hemingway's "manly"
men and "womanly" women represent a revolt against
the submergence of the individual in society. A return
to the "natural" roles and rhythms of the male-female
relationship is a way of asserting the worth of the individual in all human relationships. Hemingway is not,
however, a preacher of salvation in the Lawrence
manner. He holds out no hope of a return to Eden; his
vision remains tragic.

Brett is the center of the circle. With the exception
of Bill Gorton, all the major male characters are in love
with her—Jake, Cohn, Romero, Mike. She is not a
femme fatale or, as Cohn sees her, a Circe. She is a most
complex personality who contains many of the social
and psychological tensions of the age. Brett and Cohn
are the most believable people in the book.

Brett's "own true love" had died in the war. The
shock of that experience is presumably responsible for
her subsequent way of life. She married a man whom
she did not love and is on the way to another loveless

marriage with Mike. In Paris she presides over a hard-drinking entourage of frivolous characters. She goes away with Cohn because, as she tells Jake, she thought it would be good for him. She falls in love with Romero and beds down with him. Beyond and above all these relationships is Jake, another "true love" who in effect fulfills the function of a father confessor. She tells him all and receives his absolution.

Traditional morality is largely inoperative in Brett's life. There is an underlying recognition that she cannot resist her desires, her glands, or her whims. By no means, however, does she operate from an active principal of evil. She hurts people without meaning to. With all her sophistication, Brett comes through as a naughty little girl who requires understanding and forgiveness.

Brett struggles to hold onto some sort of moral code: she will not willfully hurt anybody. She feels sorry for Cohn when the anti-Semitic Mike is belaboring him. In her affair with Romero she even achieves, in the words of Tarrou in Camus's *The Plague*, sainthood without God. Romero wants to marry her but she decides to give him up for his own good. Tearfully she tells Jake that she will go back to Mike: "He's so damned nice and he's so awful. He's my sort of thing." Brett is pretty close to the morality of Christian renunciation.

Jake possesses all the sad knowledge of the others in the group but in a sense remains an outsider. First, as the central intelligence of the book, he passes judgment, always in the cryptic Hemingway manner, on the actions of the others. He sees the entire picture from a distance, although he remains in the picture too. Second, when Jake is by himself a loose stream-of-consciousness technique takes the reader into his mind. He is revealed as the overly sensitive Hemingway hero in the Nick Adams mold. He can give in to his weaknesses in private, but before the eyes of the world he is strong and self-possessed. Jake can be casual, even flippant about his war wound when the subject comes up in conversation. On at least one occasion, alone and in his bed after seeing Brett at the café, it is another story. He is unable to sleep and suddenly starts to cry. In the dark he is afraid when there is nobody to talk with.

Hemingway maintained a nominal allegiance to the Catholic church from the time he was married to Pauline Pfeiffer, who was a Catholic. He seems never to have needed religion in the formal sense. He tried prayer from time to time, without much success. In his fiction, however, religion and religious yearning are not uncommon features. In *A Farewell to Arms*, for example, a young priest is portrayed sympathetically. Several Hemingway heroes are vaguely seekers after God.

Jake is a Catholic. He does not so much believe in God as he *wants* to believe in God. There is a side of Jake that desperately desires and needs the church, but his disillusioned insistence on facts does not allow him to accept the peace that religion offers to some. At one point in the novel he enters a church and prays. Like Shakespeare's Claudius, his thoughts remain earthbound. He prays for everybody—Brett, Mike, Bill, Cohn, himself, the bullfighters—until he begins to feel sleepy. Then he prays that the bullfights may be good, that everybody may enjoy the fiesta, and that he may get in some good fishing. He wonders what else he should pray for and decides that he can use more money, so he prays for money. Jake's prayers may not fly upward but there is deep religious feeling in this episode as well as tough cynicism. We get the tension between an inability to believe in anything and a longing for the old certainties. Dante was able to believe that in God's will is our peace, but that was a long time ago and the Middle Ages have passed. Jake cannot let himself go to God because, in a sense, he knows too much. Jake is of his time and reflects the difficulty of accepting God in a secular age.

None of this, however, is presented academically; there are few ideologists in Hemingway. He has been accused of lacking ideas. This is true only if ideas are considered in their abstract, formal aspect. Some great novelists, Dostoyevsky, for example, often portray intellectuals whose philosophies are explicitly discussed. Another kind of novelist—Hemingway and Dickens belong here—concentrate on what the world looks like and what people do in it. The ideas are there, implicit in the action.

Like Faulkner and Joyce among the major novelists of the twentieth century, Hemingway is essentially a traditional thinker. His points of reference, his norms, are the old verities. In a world dominated by scientific thought his work centers on the emotional basis of human life. It has been said that he offers no sweeping vision for the redemption of mankind. Perhaps there have been too many sweeping visions in our time, many of them glimpsed through the lens of a microscope. It may be that facing the truth of his situation is vision enough for modern man.

Pedro Romero as hero must be distinguished from Jake Barnes. Romero is Hemingway's ideal hero, what Jake might have been in a different world. Romero is Jake without the war wound and the despair. He is unspoiled by society, since he lives among people who are close to the springs of life. He arises naturally out of a peasantry that is still simple and warm. Courage, mod-

esty, honor, confidence, all his virtues, exist by an or-
ganic necessity that requires no tortured cerebration.
He is in fact the ideal hero of the American Dream. His
real ancestors are Fenimore Cooper's Chingachgook
and Twain's Huckleberry Finn. When Brett gives him
up, she has decided to leave him uninfected by the
neurotic, overcivilized world whose disease she carries
with her.

In contrast to Cohn, Romero has no need to apologize to the universe. He fights bulls and he is good at
what he is doing. His skill is his affirmation before the
world, his mating dance before Brett, and his faith in
himself.

The Protestant work ethic is a significant component of Hemingway's respect for competence. A man
should be useful in some direction. He should do something well in his life. In all his work Hemingway expresses admiration for men who do their jobs skillfully.
Nick's father in "Indian Camp" comes to mind, and the
surgeon in *A Farewell to Arms*. Most often the admiration is focused on sportsmen, boxers, hunters, fishermen, bullfighters. He concentrates particularly on dangerous sports that require courage as well as skill and
in which ineptitude may result in physical injury or
death.

War must be included in the list of dangerous
sports. Though Hemingway voiced bitterly his disillusionment with war as an institution, he never failed to
admire the soldier who does what has to be done. It was
not a glorification of foolhardy courage, rather an appreciation of skill and stoic discipline.

Further, war experience initiates a man into certain
mysteries. He has somehow acted out the ritual of life
itself; he has faced death and come back to talk about
it. He has been accepted into an exclusive fraternity of

those who know. An honorable war wound makes one a charter member. In *The Sun Also Rises*, Count Mippipopolous, who is immediately recognized by Brett as "one of us," takes his shirt off to proudly display impressive arrow wounds that he received in Abyssinia. Colonel Richard Cantwell, in *Across the River and Into the Trees*, elevates the wound fraternity into a mystical brotherhood. Hemingway sometimes rode a hobbyhorse until it broke down.

Hemingway's feeling for skill, however, goes beyond areas of physical danger. It applies to mechanics, waiters, farmers, all people. Things should be done gracefully. He even sets great store by the skill with which a Spanish peasant drinks from a winesack. It applies to the artist equally; Hemingway disliked the dilettante writer.

Hemingway did not consider the matter in terms of the grosser forms of the American efficiency doctrine. He never gave attention to what the work ethic meant to a man on an automobile assembly line. He stopped with the craftsman orientation of nineteenth-century America. Hemingway is curiously removed from the daily lives of the ordinary men and women of his time.

At the present time, fifty years after it was published, *The Sun Also Rises* has gained rather than lost vitality. It is no longer tied to a limiting local milieu. The book clearly captures something central to twentieth-century spiritual problems. The tension between the nihilist mood and the will to believe in the old American Dream is still with us.

4

○○

Romeo
and
Juliet

On their return from Europe in 1928, the Hemingways rented an apartment in Key West for several weeks, the beginning of Ernest's long association with the Caribbean area. Late in the same year came the news of his father's suicide. Ernest was shaken by the news; he cared deeply for his father. In his *Ernest Hemingway: A Life Story*, Carlos Baker says that at the time of Ed's funeral, Ernest asked his mother "that the gun be sent to him as an historical keepsake." She complied with the request.

Hemingway had been working on a novel based on his World War I experiences in Italy. He was most anxious that it be a big, successful work that would consolidate the position he had won in the literary world with *The Sun Also Rises* and the short stories. The memory of violence and the effect of violence are the subjects of Hemingway's early work, but he did not return to the Italian war scene in an inclusive sense until *A Farewell to Arms*. He had concentrated on his youth in America and his life in postwar Europe.

The war in Italy had been a traumatic experience for the naive young man. Now, ten years after the event, sufficiently removed in time to come to artistic and emotional grips with the totality of his Italian experience, Hemingway wrote his book on the war. It is all there: the volunteer ambulance driver, the wound by the trench mortar, the hospital in Milan, Agnes von Kurowsky, Lake Maggiore, Count Greppi. It is fair to say that the book is the crystallization of the war experiences into an artistic whole that represents Hemingway's vision of man's condition in the world.

Frederic Henry, an American volunteer ambulance driver with the Italian army in World War I, leaves for duty at the front. There he suffers serious knee and leg wounds and is sent to Milan for treatment and recuperation. In the hospital he meets Catherine Barkley, a British nurse with whom he had begun a friendship before he was sent to the front. This time he falls in love with her, and the relationship is consummated in Frederic's hospital room. When he recovers, he is ordered to return to the front.

In the retreat from the Italian debacle at Caporetto, Frederic, with several companions, leaves the congested highway to try the back roads that lead to the Tagliamento River, where a new defense line is to be established. Forced to abandon his mired ambulance, he finally makes it to the bridge across the Tagliamento. He is arrested by the Italian military police, who are trying and summarily executing officers accused of deserting their troops. He breaks away from his captors and escapes by swimming the river.

Catherine rejoins him at Stresa, on the shores of Lake Maggiore. The lovers escape from Italy by rowing across the lake to Switzerland. They pass the winter happily at a mountain inn while awaiting the birth of their child. At the hospital in Lausanne a Caesarean section is performed, but the baby is stillborn, strangled by the umbilical cord. Catherine dies a few hours later. In the rain Frederic walks back to his hotel.

As a war novel, that is, in its depiction of men in battle, *A Farewell to Arms* belongs with the supreme examples of the genre. Like Stendhal in *The Charterhouse of Parma* and Crane in *The Red Badge of Courage*, Hemingway describes war as it appears in the eyes of one participant. All the confusion and formlessness of battle as it is experienced by the individual soldier comes through to the reader. Hemingway offers no panoramic view of the battleground or historical perspective of the war. He is not concerned with the strategy and tactics of commanders or statesmen.

To the men in the field, gossip and rumor take the place of overall perspective; the next meal is about as far as they can see. The mortar shell that wounds Frederic and kills Passini strikes while they are eating macaroni and cheese in a shallow dugout. Frederic hears the "chuh-chuh-chuh-chuh" just before the shell explodes, and that is all.

The retreat from Caporetto is a road choked with military vehicles heading for the banks of the Tagliamento. Sometimes Frederic and his small group do not know whether they are being shot at by Austrians or by Italians. All they know is that Aymo, one of Frederic's men, is killed by a bullet that they suspect is from an Italian rifle. German bicycle troops cross a bridge. Are they the advance guard of whole German divisions? The Italians feared German troops, and rumor had it that fifteen German divisions were joining forces with the Austrians. The reader never gets the answer; he needs none. The retreat is the retreat and no more. The texture of reality is woven by Hemingway's concentration on the foreground because life is lived in the foreground.

What comes through most clearly is the complete disillusionment with war. Frederic is distressed by the inflated rhetoric of patriotism. *Dulce et decorum est pro patria mori* is humbug to the man who faces death in battle. The soldiers do not seek political or moral justification; they want to get out of the war alive.

Hemingway shows war to be an intolerable affront to humanity, but he is not centrally concerned with the political aspects of war. The book is Frederic Henry's farewell to arms, not the world's. This is not to say that Hemingway is unaware of political undercurrents. The soldiers grumble against the leaders who sent them off to war. "Down with the officers" is heard on the shores of the Tagliamento. The men want peace, not victory. Hemingway's recognition of political problems, however, does not extend to ideological commitment; *A Farewell to Arms* is not propaganda. He knows too much about men to divide them into good guys and bad guys according to their politics or country of origin. The rebellious Italian soldiers are a vicious lot, ready to attack any officer; Frederic himself is in danger because he is a lieutenant. The military police question their victims with "all the efficiency, coldness and command of themselves of Italians who are firing and are not being fired on."

Hemingway detests cruelty and cowardice and self-delusion. He goes by a complex feeling for decency that is composed of elements drawn from sources as divergent as the fair-play doctrine in sports and Christian teaching. In an age of ideology, Hemingway the artist chose men over any ideology; he refused to be drawn into excessive abstraction. In the twentieth-century welter of ideology and sloganizing, Hemingway always held back something of himself. He never allowed himself or his art to be submerged in a social or political movement.

As we shall see, when Hemingway, in the 1930s, did make a political commitment to the Spanish Loyalists against Franco, his novel on that subject, *For Whom the Bell Tolls*, infuriated the communists, then participating in the war against the fascists. The communists failed to understand that Hemingway's support of the popular front did not mean that he had rejected his belief that cruelty is cruelty no matter where it is found, and that men are more often trapped by what is false within than by false ideology. Hemingway was not cut out for political propaganda.

A Farewell to Arms shows Hemingway's style at

its full maturity. It is strange that this should be so since
Hemingway was only thirty years old when the book
was published. It is nevertheless true that no later novel
of Hemingway is quite so sharply incised, so well-
controlled. Ironically, the overwhelming critical and
popular acclaim that greeted *A Farewell to Arms* may
have had something to do with the decline of Hemingway's stylistic purity: henceforth Hemingway was to
write with full consciousness of himself, his standing in
the literary world, his legend. His subsequent work
began, on occasion, to *imitate*, some would say *caricature*, Hemingway.

In *A Farewell to Arms* the terse dialogue is handled
with complete confidence. Conversation is presented in
almost pure dramatic form without the assistance of
clumsy signposts—the "he said" and "she rejoined mer-
rily" convention—which the traditional novel used and
which Hemingway had not completely eradicated from
the short stories and *The Sun Also Rises*. Hemingway's
handling of dialogue in *A Farewell to Arms* is a tri-
umph of immediacy; the reader is *there*. Nothing superfluous distracts the reader from the scene itself.

The descriptive passages concentrate on the most
significant physical elements without becoming over-
detailed. Hemingway never forgets his story in favor
of self-indulgent lingering over an object that lends
itself to verbal embellishment.

In *A Farewell to Arms* Hemingway reduces further his use of descriptive adjectives. The nouns, if anything, become simpler than in his earlier work. There
is no straining for the unusual or spectacular verbal
effect. The outlines of the images are not sharply cut;
the technique, rather, is impressionistic in that the
reader focuses the image by combining the colors for

himself. Hemingway shows his consummate artistry in knowing when not to say more.

The opening lines of the novel offer a good example of Hemingway's controlled descriptive power:

In the late summer of that year we lived in a house in a village that looked across the river and the plain to the mountains. In the bed of the river there were pebbles and boulders, dry and white in the sun, and the water was clear and swiftly moving and blue in the channels. Troops went by the house and down the road and the dust they raised powdered the leaves of the trees.

Like Samuel Johnson's Imlac in *Rasselas*, Hemingway "does not number the streaks of the tulip." A house is a house, an orchard an orchard.

As a storytelling technique Hemingway's spare prose fulfills yet another function. The reader immediately and without question trusts the narrator, Frederic, to give an objective view. The style makes it clear that he is not trying to embellish the story, aggrandize his own role, or force his interpretations on the reader. In fact, he seems to be trying to keep himself in the background. Only in rare instances does the reticence of the narrator fail to hold. When that happens it is because Hemingway himself tends to take over and the distinction between author and narrator is blurred. Near the end of the book, when Frederic thinks about his dead child and about Catherine, who is near death, he compares life to a baseball game into which they threw you before you had mastered the rules. He recalls the ants swarming out of a log that he had put on a campfire. The ants destroyed themselves in their blind frenzy to escape destruction. The reader suspects that this dark picture of the human condition is more Hemingway than Frederic, even to the choice of examples. In his

later work Hemingway increasingly put himself into
his characters so that he seemed to be defending his
private life. In *A Farewell to Arms* such shortening of
distance between author and work is the exception.

With an easy inevitability the justly admired opening chapter of *A Farewell to Arms* sets the emotional
tone of the book, a foreboding of doom. In two short
pages Hemingway sketches in the physical background
of his story, the plains and hills of northern Italy in
war. He takes us from late summer through the fall to
winter. The winter rain, a symbol of death and disaster
throughout the book, closes the short chapter: "At the
start of the winter came the permanent rain and with
the rain came the cholera. But it was checked and in
the end only seven thousand died of it in the army."
The irony of this last sentence prepares the reader
emotionally for what follows in the book.

A Farewell to Arms has a tragic intensity that is
not found in *The Sun Also Rises*. In the earlier book
the atmosphere of spiritual defeat blankets everything.
Jake's love for Brett is hopeless from the beginning.
The Brett-Romero liaison is not developed sufficiently
by Hemingway to arouse full tragic emotion in the
reader. Brett seems to be off on another exercise in
promiscuity; Romero never quite becomes a flesh and
blood figure. The possibilities for genuine tragic emotion are not sustained; the pathetic ingredient pre-
dominates.

In *A Farewell to Arms*, however, Hemingway
presents a successful, even an ideal love that is consummated and that, it must be assumed, would have
endured had it not been abruptly terminated by death.
Edmund Wilson reported that Hemingway had re-
ferred to the book as his *Romeo and Juliet*.

A Farewell to Arms achieves the emotional intensity of tragedy but it is the attenuated tragedy of the twentieth century. In Hemingway the affirmation of life that is to be found in even the most bitter of Shakespeare's tragedies is shrunken. The affirmation is there, nevertheless, in the love of Frederic and Catherine. If it is not the paean to love that we find in *Romeo and Juliet* it is because we do not live in Elizabethan England. Shakespeare's awareness of the void was balanced by an equal awareness of the richness of life.

In Hemingway, the balance is tilted toward the void, but his heroes are not without a capacity for life. There is a significant difference between Hemingway and the more thoroughgoing nihilists of our age, Beckett, let us say. One cannot conceive of *Waiting for Godot* with a pair of true lovers sitting under the leafless tree. In Hemingway, the leaves still grow and the lovers may be happy although their happiness is doomed to early destruction. His lovers never get to test their love through a long mortgage in suburbia. In the affirmative aspects of his approach to experience, he is essentially a romantic. It is either a hopeless dream of love that he focuses on, or a short-lived actuality destroyed by a malevolent universe. The destructive forces do not necessarily have a basis in the individual. The catastrophe may come gratuitously, not as in the classic tragedy through flaws inherent in the virtues of the hero.

Catherine's death has no causal connection with anything that has gone before in the book. Safe with her lover in Switzerland after their escape from Italy, she dies in childbirth. The war itself is not responsible for her death unless one stretches the meaning of causality to a point where all distinctions are blurred. In Aristotelean terms the accidents of biology, Catherine's bodily structure in this instance, are possible but not probable. *Romeo and Juliet,* a tragedy of fate or chance, may also be seen as culminating in a gratuitous calamity, but that calamity is solidly grounded in the family feud.

A Farewell to Arms is desperate tragedy in that it makes an affirmation in an essentially hopeless world. In Hemingway we encounter the complexities of the modern sensibility: the heart wars with the head. Hemingway does not reject the instinctive life forces, no matter how dark his rational evaluation of life. His faith in human potentiality is never rejected, nor is his feeling that life can give many joys.

On its own ground *A Farewell to Arms* is one of the great love stories in American literature. Hemingway's capacity for tenderness has not been sufficiently acknowledged. When the lovers first meet, they play what Catherine calls "this rotten game." Frederic professes a love that he does not feel although Catherine, with all her weary cynicism, seems to sense something deeper in her feeling for him. In the Milan hospital the wounded Frederic comes to understand that he is in love with Catherine. She may not be the ideal Women's Liberation heroine, but she is all woman. Her capacity for giving happiness to her lover is boundless. She is as tender, trusting, and protective as Juliet. When she tells Frederic that she is afraid of the rain because she sometimes sees herself dead in it, he tries to reassure her by saying that it is more likely that he may be dead in the rain. She denies the possibility: "Because I can keep you safe. I know I can. But nobody can help themselves." Catherine feels that she is doomed but that she can somehow protect Frederic. She expresses the stoicism, the Christianity, the heroism, the romanticism, and the sentimentalism that in unlikely combination comprise Hemingway's world view.

Hemingway's forthright depiction and discussion of matters sexual shocked American readers, but it must be recalled that those were the years when *Lady Chatterley's Lover* was adjudged pornographic by the courts. In *A Farewell to Arms* the lovers are unmarried, although Catherine considers herself to be as married as any woman ever was. In Switzerland, Frederic suggests that they go through with the formal ceremony before the child is born. Catherine prefers to wait because the marriage would be embarrassing since she is obviously pregnant. It is she who convinces Frederic to delay the marriage until she is thin again. Marriage remains the norm, with its formal aspects made light of but never rejected.

Frederic's closest friend is the surgeon, Lieutenant Rinaldi, a mercurial cynic and mocker of the ideal, yet a good man who is brought to the breaking point by the suffering with which he must contend as a war doctor. He believes that he has contracted syphilis, an "industrial accident" as he calls it. Outside of his work he finds nothing to hold his interest except drinking and whoring. Knowledge of the world has destroyed Rinaldi's capacity for intuitive living. He asserts that he knows more than Frederic but that he will not enjoy life as much. It is true. Frederic can still hear the faint music of the spheres through the static. The Hemingway heroes never finally reject life.

The military chaplain, a young Catholic priest from Abruzzi, has a significant role in the novel. From the outset he is the object of merciless baiting by the officers. A foul-mouthed captain leads the attack; later, Rinaldi takes over in a somewhat gentler vein. Frederic is an interested observer, but he does not actively participate in the baiting. The priest senses a muted sympathy in Frederic. When Frederic is about to go on leave, the priest invites him to go to the Abruzzi and visit his family. Abruzzi is a mountainous region in central Italy on the Adriatic Sea, noteworthy for its simple peasant life and its clear, cold climate. Frederic promises to go but instead makes the rounds of the big cities. On his return, he recalls dispiritedly the routine of smoky cafés, wine, girls, and mornings after. He reflects that he had actually intended to go to the Abruzzi, that he had visited "no place where the roads were frozen and hard as iron, where it was clear cold and dry and the snow was dry and powdery and hare-tracks in the snow and the peasants took off their hats and called you Lord and there was good hunting." Significantly, when Frederic passes the winter with Catherine in the Swiss mountains above Montreux, he finally, at least in a spiritual sense, gets to the Abruzzi.

In the field hospital the wounded Frederic is visited by the priest who makes a hesitant effort to convert him to Catholicism. He does not succeed. The Hemingway hero can never accept a clean-cut religious affirmation. The priest talks about himself. He looks forward to the time when the war will be over and he can return to the Abruzzi: "There in my country it is understood that a man may love God. It is not a dirty joke." In Frederic's mind the young priest becomes part of a complex symbol of everything good. Like Jake Barnes, Frederic wants to believe but cannot or will not let himself. He sees too many other sides of the question. In a further discussion with the priest, Frederic says that it is only in defeat that men become Christians, that is, meek and gentle after the model of Jesus.

Frederic makes no final commitment to the views of either the priest or Rinaldi. Clearly he is closer to Rinaldi as a human being than he is to the priest. Yet the priest stands up much better than Rinaldi. In the stress of war he does not break down. When Frederic rejoins his unit after his recuperation in Milan, he notes that the priest is unchanged while the others, particularly Rinaldi, show obvious signs of strain.

Hemingway is able to stand away from his characters and from himself to give us a rich, complex picture of the unresolved conflict between denial and affirmation in our time. He supplies a summation and a coda in the conversation between Frederic and Count Greffi over a game of billiards in the hotel at Stresa, where he and Catherine are staying before their escape across the lake to Switzerland. Greffi, an aged nobleman of great charm, talks with Frederic about life and death, God and love. When he asks Frederic whether he is a believer, the familiar Hemingway answer is given: "At night." Greffi himself has become less devout as he has grown older, but he is hardly the advocate against God. He even seems to encourage belief, pointing out that Frederic is in love and "that is a religious feeling."

5

○○

Bulls
and
Kudus

Nine years elapsed between the publication of *A Farewell to Arms* and Hemingway's next novel. Two major works of nonfiction were published during this period, *Death in the Afternoon* in 1932 and *The Green Hills of Africa* in 1935, in addition to numerous short stories of high quality.

In the 1930s Hemingway increasingly became involved in controversy with critics and reviewers. During that period, criticism of Hemingway's work was not notable for depth or fairness; many critics never looked beyond the visible surface of Hemingway's art. It was variously said that he was in a rut, that he had written himself out, that he was merely a sportswriter, that he dealt only with violence, that he had succumbed to fame and was grinding out lucrative potboilers rather than creative literature. The last charge was partly true: Hemingway's topical articles and reportage for the better-paying magazines, *Esquire* for instance, were often unworthy of his position in American letters. Hemingway noted in reply that an artist is ultimately judged by his best work.

Death in the Afternoon is a textbook and history of bullfighting in Spain, including a glossary and an excellent selection of photographs that Hemingway had collected. Any book on this subject is a rarity in English. *Death in the Afternoon* has the additional distinction of being sound in scholarship and, not unexpectedly, readable. From his first attendance at a bullfight during the postwar years in Europe, Hemingway discovered that he was not revolted, as he had anticipated he would be, by the cruelty of the spectacle. He was attracted by the aesthetic and spiritual values of the bullfight.

He became an *aficionado*, that is, passionate about bullfights. In Hemingway's own words, "the *aficio-*

nado; or lover of the bullfight, may be said, broadly
. . . to be one who has this sense of the tragedy and
ritual of the fight so that the minor aspects are not
important except as they relate to the whole." The bullfighter himself may or may not be an *aficionado*. If he
approaches his work with a feeling for its transcendent
significance and for the dignity of his own role he
becomes an *aficionado*.

In the north of Europe and in the United States,
the bullfight has generally been regarded with disgust
as a display of cruelty and barbarity. From one point
of view *Death in the Afternoon* was Hemingway's attempt to convince his countrymen of their error.

Each bull in the fight is engaged in a kind of drama
consisting of three acts. The function of acts one and
two is to prepare the bull for death by the sword of
the matador in act three. First the picador, mounted on
a horse and armed with a long lance, and then the
banderillero, armed with steel-pointed barbs, weaken
the bull in order to restrict his range of movement.

It is in the first act of the bullfight that the horses
(usually old and slow) ridden by the picadors are
sometimes ripped open or killed by the horns of the
bull. The charge of cruelty is most often leveled against
this feature, especially by newcomers to the bullfight.

The final act is the killing of the bull by the matador, who, at great danger to himself, must deliver the
sword thrust from above, between the shoulder blades
of the bull.

Hemingway sees the bullfight as a ritual tragedy
rather than a sport or spectacle: the bull is sure to die.
In the broadest view, *Death in the Afternoon* seeks to
establish an analogy between the bullfight and the human predicament. The bullfighter or the bull, or both,
somehow come to represent the central experience of

mankind, the confrontation with death. Hemingway is close to the existentialists in his gnawing awareness of man's precarious position: death is possible at any time, inevitable in the end. Hemingway, of course, is most interested in violent death, a fact that sets him apart from the existentialists.

A genuine tragic emotion may be communicated to the spectator by the drama of the bullfighter courageously facing the bull and showing his contempt for death, and of the bull's inevitable death. At "the moment of truth," when man and bull merge in the ritual of death, a return to the mythic sources of tragedy is achieved.

In *The Sun Also Rises*, Jake Barnes tells Cohn that "nobody ever lives their life all the way up except the bullfighters." Hemingway undoubtedly romanticizes the role of the bullfighter in *Death in the Afternoon*. On the art of killing bulls, for example, he asserts that the bullfighter

must have a spiritual enjoyment of the moment of killing. Killing cleanly and in a way which gives you aesthetic pleasure and pride has always been one of the greatest enjoyments of a part of the human race. . . . When a man is still in rebellion against death he has pleasure in taking to himself one of the Godlike attributes; that of giving it.

Hemingway is being carried away by his own mystique of the hunter, which he put to much better use in "The Short Happy Life of Francis Macomber."

In the seventh chapter of *Death in the Afternoon* Hemingway introduces a fictional character in the person of the Old Lady, with whom the author discusses bullfights and all manner of relevant and irrelevant subjects at intervals through the rest of the book. Even without the Old Lady, Hemingway contrived to introduce short narratives, anecdotes, and sketches, but her presence made variety easier to achieve. It is as though the straitjacket of the textbook format was beginning to cramp Hemingway's style and he decided to seek the relative freedom of fiction. Through the device of the Old Lady, Hemingway comments casually on the facts, airs his prejudices, caricatures the opposition, philosophizes, or makes jokes as the fancy strikes him.

The basic factual orientation and sobriety of *Death in the Afternoon* is not seriously vitiated by the romanticism that Hemingway occasionally introduces into his account. A man who loved a land as much as Hemingway did Spain, and who had so many memories of glorious experiences in that land may be allowed his romanticisms. Since Hemingway believed that the bullfight was a profound expression of the Spanish people, *Death in the Afternoon* becomes more than a book on the bullfight. It is also cultural history, a solid travel book, and something of a love song to Spain.

Late in 1933, the Hemingways, accompanied by Charles Thompson, Ernest's close friend and fishing companion from Key West, undertook a long-planned safari to East Africa for big-game hunting. The trip was a great success; Hemingway loved Africa. On the literary side, the safari supplied Hemingway with the material for *Green Hills of Africa* and for two of his finest short stories, "The Short Happy Life of Francis Macomber" and "The Snows of Kilimanjaro."

As he tells us in the foreword to *Green Hills of Africa*, Hemingway was trying something new:

Unlike many novels, none of the characters in this book is imaginary. Any one not finding sufficient love interest, is at liberty, while reading it, to insert whatever love interest he or she may have at the time. The writer has attempted to write an absolutely true book to see whether the shape of a country and the pattern of a month's action can, if truly presented, compete with a work of the imagination.

Outside of changing the names of the Europeans and Americans on the safari—Charles Thompson is Karl, the white hunter Philip Percival is Pop, Pauline Hemingway is P.O.M.—nothing fictional is introduced. It must be acknowledged, of course, that no writing, even newspaper reporting, can reproduce an event in all its details and nuances. Some selection must be made from the endless tangle of lived experience. Yet, allowing the metaphysical impossibility of deciding precisely what reality consists of, *Green Hills of Africa* is life as actually lived, an attempt to say it as it was without the organizing of experience that is associated with fiction. As factual narrative, the book is remarkably successful. Although he came to love Africa as much as he loved Spain, very little of the romanticism of *Death in the Afternoon* shows up in the work. A man almost always looks back on the experiences of his younger days through a romantic screen.

In his fiction Hemingway succeeded in capturing the immediate truth of objects, situations, and events so that the reader is there. Hemingway did not *tell* a story; he *dramatized* it. He did no less for East Africa in a nonfictional account. The Serengetti Plain with its vast herds of zebra, wildebeest, and antelope comes through with a special definition that distinguishes it from the equally special Big Two-Hearted River, the grove of beeches at Burguete, or Lake Maggiore in the winter darkness.

The ability to establish a sense of place is among Hemingway's most valuable literary assets. He managed to give us Michigan or Africa, not merely a campfire in the wilds. The smell of animals, the dried sweat of hunters at the end of a day in the sun, the taste of meat cooked over a campfire, the feel of an oiled gun barrel, the sound of a bullet hitting the hide of a rhinoceros, the giggling of a native guide—all are given a tight local habitation. In the twentieth century only D. H. Lawrence rivals Hemingway as a travel writer. Hemingway's honesty with the facts of experience results in immediacy of experience for the reader.

The pattern of the "month's action" did not restrict Hemingway to a purely chronological sequence. By use of a flashback technique operating through the consciousness of the narrator, Hemingway himself in this case, events prior to the month's action are recounted.

In dialogue and descriptive power, there is little difference between *Green Hills of Africa* and Hemingway's fiction. Even the preferences and prejudices of the fictional heroes are duplicated, understandably, by Hemingway in his own person—mountain over plain, cool weather over hot, honesty over self-deception, the natural over the decadent.

The pattern of the month's action, truly presented as Hemingway planned, does not quite come up to the level of Hemingway's imaginative fiction. This is not to say that *Green Hills of Africa* is not successful. In a work of imagination, the artist shapes people and events to produce a unified emotional impact of significant consequence in men's lives. He gives direction to truth so that it comes out "more true." The imagined world of the artist is more real, in a sense, than the experiences he draws upon from so-called real life.

Hemingway undoubtedly gave some direction to *Green Hills of Africa*. The substantial organizing principles are the competition between Hemingway and Karl, and the climactic hunt for the bull kudu. Neither of these themes is sufficiently developed to generate the deepest emotional involvement in the reader. One thinks of *The Old Man and the Sea* and what Hemingway did with an old fisherman who was competitive and wanted to catch the biggest fish, or with the stories that grew imaginatively out of the African safari.

Philip Percival, Pop in *Green Hills of Africa*, was transformed into the white hunter, Wilson, in the Macomber story. Pop, the professional leader of the safari, commands respect because he knows his job thoroughly and does it without any posturing for effect. He is a good man to have alongside if your rifle shot wounds the lion just enough to make him more dangerous. A man of few words and much wisdom, he serves as an individualized Greek chorus, commenting on and keeping in perspective the actions of the narrator who, of course, passes judgment on all the people, whites and natives, in the book, including Pop. But Pop laconically passes judgment on Hemingway, whose competitive spirit and occasional bragging about his skill as tracker and shooter come in for humorous or severe criticism. Pop is the Supreme Court of the safari.

Although it is clear that Hemingway is objectively and often ironically recording his own failings, it is Pop who makes the explicit criticism. When Karl's kudu turns out to have a much larger pair of horns than Hemingway's, Hemingway is obviously bitter though he tries to cover it. After a night's sleep he feels better and more charitable, or so he says. Without conviction, Hemingway tells Pop that he is really glad that Karl has the better trophy. Pop, gently but without pussy-footing, says the final word: "We have very primitive emotions. . . . It's impossible not to be competitive. Spoils everything, though."

Hemingway's portraits of the native members of the safari individualize each one. He sketches some in short, broad strokes; others are drawn in detail. M'Cola, who is a major character, is a regular employee on Pop's jobs. He is Hemingway's gun-bearer; they become great friends.

On the trail after kudu, the party hires a local tracker given to the theatrical and to ostentatious authority. Hemingway dislikes him and assigns him the name Garrick, after the famous English actor of the eighteenth century. To the delectation of M'Cola and himself, Hemingway manages to contrive Garrick's comeuppance. But he is given his due: he is an acceptable guide and tracker.

Hemingway gives us a warm, affectionate picture of the handsome, good-natured Masai warriors, who race the car as it leaves for the hunt, and, on its return, eat the party's bread, mince meat, and plum pudding in a holiday spirit.

The successive encounters with the lion, the water buffalo, and the rhinoceros are disappointing to the safari. They lack the tension and drama that had been expected: the lion does not charge, the buffalo seems slow and helpless, and the rhinoceros is pitiful in its ugliness. The kudu hunt is more satisfying because Hemingway sees the kudu as a clean and noble animal, and because kudu horns are spectacular enough to excite the imagination.

The Hemingway code for killing game becomes a judgment of the universe and a moral position. Again, one must kill cleanly. To allow a wounded animal to escape is to condemn the animal to prolonged suffering and to endanger any passer-by who may stumble into the path of the animal. Morality dictates that the hunter must seek out and kill the wounded animal even at the greatest danger to himself.

It is not easy to define with precision Hemingway's moral distinctions between different species of animals. Some are noble and good; they may kill in order to live but that is the way of nature. The good animals live by their courage, skill, or speed. They are graceful and handsome, aesthetically satisfying.

Then there are the evil animals—hyenas, sharks, snakes, insects—that live by stealing from the labor of others, or are cowardly, or treacherous, or simply annoying. The distinction between good and bad animals may not be fair to the animals and may not add up to sound zoology or ecology, but it served Hemingway's moral code. The feeling for honor and beauty, for a basic decency, is instinctive in Hemingway. It rests on a profound respect for all life in the midst of death and killing. Quite illogically, then, Hemingway has his villains in the animal world, and it must be added, in the human world. In "The Snows of Kilimanjaro," the dying writer remembers that during his war days in Italy an officer named Barker "had flown across the lines to bomb the Austrian officers' leave train, machine-gunning them as they scattered and ran" and that one of his comrades had called him a "bloody murderous bastard."

In the first chapter of *Green Hills of Africa* Hemingway engages in an extended literary conversation with an Austrian plantation manager named Kandinsky. Kandinsky turns the discussion to American writing. Hemingway believes that even the good writers of the nineteenth century in America—that is, those who found "how things, actual things, can be"—Melville, for example, insulated their writing with so much rhetoric that it became difficult for a reader to get at the things. As for the New England group, "Emerson, Hawthorne, Whittier, and Company," they suffered from gentility. "They did not use the words that people always have used in speech, the words that survive in language. Nor would you gather that they had bodies. They had minds, yes. Nice, dry, clean minds."

The good writers are Henry James, Stephen Crane, and Mark Twain (not in that order, Hemingway warns). For Twain he stakes out a tremendous claim: "All modern American literature comes from one book by Mark Twain called *Huckleberry Finn*. . . . It's the best book we've had. All American writing comes from that. There was nothing before. There has been nothing as good since."

Hemingway leaves Africa with the intention of returning: "I knew a good country when I saw one. Here there was game, plenty of birds, and I liked the natives. Here I could shoot and fish. That, and writing, and reading, and seeing pictures was all I cared about doing"—not an earthshaking thought but solid enough and, above all, honest.

6

○○

Artistry
in the
Short
Story

By 1938 Hemingway had forty-nine short stories to his credit. Two volumes of stories had followed *In Our Time*. In 1927 *Men without Women* was published; in 1933, *Winner Take Nothing*. The vision and method established in the early stories remain substantially unchanged, although with maturity Hemingway penetrates even more deeply into the emotional and spiritual lives of his people. The visible action of the stories continues to take place in the foreground; the invisible reaches far back into the realm of the human spirit.

Nick Adams reappears in several stories, now being treated at a rehabilitation center in Milan, now emotionally disturbed on a new assignment at the front, now an older man and a father trying to explain to his son why they have never visited the grave of Nick's father. The real subject matter of these stories is the vague longing of the human heart for understanding. The least vague of writers, Hemingway always wrestles with the vague and the intangible.

Subtle relationships between men and women are explored in the stories: a girl and her lover discuss her coming abortion; a woman leaves her lover in order to live with a lesbian; a married couple return to Paris to set up separate residences. Always there is more to these stories than there seems to be.

"A Clean, Well-Lighted Place," one of Hemingway's own favorites, deals with the *nada* concept, the overwhelming sense of emptiness that hangs over our age. An old, deaf man sits drinking in a café late into the night. A young waiter, anxious to close up and go home, pressures the old man into leaving. Another waiter, older, tries to explain the need of the old man for a clean, well-lighted place. The old man had recently attempted suicide. The young waiter is insensitive and argues that the old man can drink at home just as conveniently. "It's not the same" answers the second waiter. They finally close for the night. The older waiter stops at a bar for a drink before heading home.

He disliked bars and bodegas. A clean, well-lighted café was a very different thing. Now, without thinking further, he would go home to his room. He would lie in the bed and finally, with daylight, he would go to sleep. After all, he said to himself, it is probably only insomnia. Many must have it.

This is Hemingway at his best. In five pages, he gives us the lineaments of our time and the suggestion of the human condition in any time. And all this is effected without moving away from the narrow spotlight of the café. Here is all life's loneliness, compassion, love, need of people for other people, as well as cruelty and insensitivity. It is the overpowering unsaid that is the heart of the story. The well-known parody of the Lord's Prayer, strikingly effective in itself, may be the only weakness in the story.

Our nada who art in nada, nada be thy name thy kingdom nada thy will be nada in nada as it is in nada. Give us this nada our daily nada and nada us our nada as we nada our nadas and nada us not into nada but deliver us from nada.

The older waiter, in whose mind the parody is revolving, seems out of character in this bitter philosophic rumination. It is difficult to resist the conclusion that Hemingway is in his own person offering editorial comment. It would appear that Hemingway could not resist throwing in what is surely by itself a powerful statement. It is, however, a superfluous intrusion into a story that stands on its own strong feet.

The two stories that grew out of the African safari,

"The Short Happy Life of Francis Macomber" and "The Snows of Kilimanjaro," achieved the status of classics during their author's lifetime. The voluminous criticism of these stories, however, has by no means exhausted the subject. The possibilities for further analysis and interpretation are endless.

Francis Macomber, a wealthy American in his middle thirties, and his wife, Margot, are on a hunting safari in East Africa led by Robert Wilson, an experienced professional guide. Macomber wounds a lion, which hides in the tall grass. Wilson insists that they go after the lion though the operation is extremely dangerous. Reluctantly, and admitting his fear, Macomber accompanies Wilson. When the lion charges, Macomber bolts and runs, leaving Wilson to kill the lion. From the car, Macomber's cowardly behavior is seen in its entirety by Margot. She mercilessly pillories her husband. On the trip back to camp she leans over from the rear seat of the car to kiss Wilson on the mouth. In the middle of the night she leaves her husband asleep and goes to Wilson's tent, where she remains for several hours. On her return, she quarrels bitterly with Macomber, who had been awake for some time.

Macomber does not evade the issue of his cowardice. He openly admits that he bolted "like a rabbit." After a talk with Wilson, Macomber feels that he has recovered his courage; he looks forward eagerly to the buffalo hunt. Macomber, in a situation that duplicates that of the lion hunt, redeems himself by unhesitatingly going after a wounded buffalo. With Wilson he stands firm and fires away at the charging animal. At that moment, Margot, from some distance, fires at the buffalo. Her bullet hits the back of Macomber's head, killing him instantly.

"The Short Happy Life of Francis Macomber,"
considered as simply a hunting yarn, achieves a high
level of suspense and emotional intensity. Ironically,
Macomber dies after only a few hours as a man of
courage; his rebirth is the prelude to his final demise.
But this is much more than a hunting yarn, although it
is that, too. It is a story that examines the elemental
bases of the male-female relationship and the sources of
human freedom and dependence.

The most popular reading of the story concludes,
as Wilson clearly concludes, that Margot shot her husband because she knew that a courageous Macomber
would leave her. The courage to face a charging buffalo is presumably the courage to face anything. In this
approach, no allowance is made for the possibility that
Margot intended to help her husband in his peril and
accidentally killed him. It is a good reading, including
as it does the complex interplay between the beautiful
woman and the wealthy man whose eleven-year marriage has been on the verge of dissolution several times,
a marriage that seems to have survived because each
partner thinks he may not be able to do better. The
marriage is held together by fear and insecurity rather
than anything positive.

With the burden of his cowardice upon him, Macomber sinks even lower by begging Wilson not to tell
other people how he had acted. When Macomber recovers his courage, Wilson is frankly bewildered by
the change:

> Look at the beggar now, Wilson thought. Sometimes
> all their lives. Their figures stay boyish when they're fifty.
> The great American boy-men. Damned strange people. But
> he liked this Macomber now. Damned strange fellow.
> Probably meant the end of cuckoldry too.

Another reading is made possible by calling into question the moral authority of Wilson. It is usually assumed that Wilson represents the viewpoint that Hemingway intended the reader to be guided by, but a careful reading raises some doubt. First, Wilson sees nothing wrong in cuckolding Macomber. He carries a double size cot on safari so that he can take advantage of windfalls. He adopts the moral standards of his clientele in all except hunting, a neat trick.

It is Wilson who labels Margot an out and out bitch and, in effect, charges her with the murder of her husband. The evidence in the story itself is far from conclusive on that point. It should be noted, too, that when Margot charges him with breaking the game laws by pursuing the buffalo from the car, he, like Macomber earlier, asks her not to report the incident, since it would cost him his license. Macomber smiles and remarks to Wilson, "Now she has something on you."

When Wilson becomes aware that Macomber knows of his liaison with Margot, he hopes that "the silly beggar doesn't take a notion to blow the back of my head off." A pretty strong case can be made for Wilson's moral limitations. His attitude to women is extremely cynical: the only way to handle them is to dominate completely.

No matter which reading one prefers, the essential value of the story remains intact; namely, the penetrating insight into the delicate emotional balance that enters into the relationship between a man and a woman.

"The Snows of Kilimanjaro" begins with an explanatory epigraph:

Kilimanjaro is a snow covered mountain 19,710 feet high, and is said to be the highest mountain in Africa. Its western summit is called the Masai "Ngaje Ngai," the

House of God. Close to the western summit there is the dried and frozen carcass of a leopard. No one has explained what the leopard was seeking at that altitude.

The story consists of the thoughts, feverish recollections, and fantasies of a writer dying of a gangrene infection while on a hunting trip in East Africa. His wife tries to comfort him, to no avail; he knows he is dying. Their own truck has broken down and neither the expected rescue truck or plane has arrived.

Harry tries to evaluate his life. He feels that he has fallen short of what he might have accomplished as an artist. His wife's money has helped destroy his talent. He notes that whenever he fell in love, the woman had more money than the last woman had. He liked the comfort of not having to write. Finally, he did no work at all. He destroyed his talent by not using it, by drink, by sheer laziness. The memories flood in upon him—so much to write about, better than anything he had ever written. No time now.

At last a light plane flown by a bush pilot arrives to take him to the hospital. The plane takes off safely but instead of following the proper course for Nairobi, swings off to the left. "There, ahead, all he could see, as wide as the world, great, high, and unbelievably white in the sun, was the square top of Kilimanjaro. And then he knew that there was where he was going." The plane had never really come to rescue the writer. He lay dead in his tent.

It is tempting, and too easy, to read "The Snows of Kilimanjaro" as autobiography. On his African safari, Hemingway came down with amoebic dysentery and was flown to Nairobi by a bush pilot. The plane passed within sight of Kilimanjaro.

A great disservice and injustice is done to Hemingway and to the story if it is read as a straight personal

confession. It is quite another matter, however, to recognize that this *is* a very personal story, obviously close
in many details to Hemingway's life. It should be said
that Hemingway was expressing many of the ambiguities and doubts he felt about his own life and work, and
about the problems of American writers in general.
Even the story's final affirmation of the writer's im-
mortality should not be construed as Hemingway's
confidence in the significance of his own writing.

The story reaches out beyond the problems of the
artist. Perhaps it is best read as the feeling of any man
at the point of death, reviewing the meaning of his
life—what he had accomplished, where he had failed,
where succeeded, and, yes, what might be left on earth
of his spirit after his death.

7

○○

No Man
Is an Island

The great depression of the 1930s, introduced by a startling stock-market crash, quickly dispelled the hysterical gaiety of the 1920s. America was in serious trouble. The patriotic call for a rebirth of rugged individualism sounded like a bad joke to the millions of unemployed. Clearly it was a time for rethinking the old philosophies by which the country had prospered and achieved greatness. It must be remembered that unemployment insurance and social security benefits were still in the future. The extensive social legislation of the New Deal, under the leadership of Franklin D. Roosevelt, did not have a decisive effect until the second half of the decade.

Leftist ideologies, all in some measure calling for the social and technological reorganization of economic life, made tremendous advances. The Communist party became a major force in American politics. Holding up the successful Russian Revolution as a model and Stalin as the ideal leader, the communists insisted that the artist put his talents to work on behalf of the working class. In a time of widespread suffering among millions of Americans, the artist must not withdraw to the ivory tower of aestheticism and neutralism. As the communists saw it, the problem of the artist was not to describe the world but to change it. He must use his art to help the people achieve a better social order. Art was to become a weapon in the revolutionary struggle. Mike Gold, editor of *New Masses*, called for "proletarian realism." In effect, artists were to be measured and evaluated by their usefulness as political propagandists for the party line.

Hemingway's position as the country's outstanding literary artist made him a favorite target of the leftist critics. It was reiterated that in the midst of overwhelming social disaster, Hemingway indulged in frivolous pursuits. His books, it was charged, were concerned either with these personal interests or with characters who were the disillusioned and parasitic dregs of society. His heroes were isolated and alienated individuals seeking an impossible individual salvation. It was said that his compassion should logically bring him to join forces with the progressive working class. Instead, he frittered away his life and art in narcissistic indulgence.

The attacks on Hemingway, however, were never so vitriolic that the door to conversion was not left unlocked. The leftists knew that he was a rich prize: Hemingway in their camp would be a symbol of the national surge leftward and an encouragement to other writers and intellectuals to join the movement. The communists recognized that Hemingway was in no sense an enemy of the working masses. In fact, his sympathies were generally with the beaten and the exploited, although he never accepted the rigid, simplistic class lines drawn by communist ideology.

Some aspects of Hemingway's art could not be faulted by the communists. His literary method stressed truth and honesty; he could not be charged with the sort of genteel approach to American life that Mike Gold, in his famous article in the *New Republic*, attacked in Thornton Wilder.

Hemingway's works were very popular in the Soviet Union, much more so than the ephemeral so-called proletarian novels then being written in America by Albert Halper, Josephine Herbst, Jack Conroy, and Grace Lumpkin. *A Farewell to Arms* implicitly expressed a revulsion from, and a disillusionment with, war, features that reinforced the communist characterization of World War I as an imperialist war. What Hemingway might do with a war favored by the left was, of course, another question. He was not one to deliver political sermons on the distinction between imperialist wars and wars of national liberation.

His compassion for the suffering of the common people was undeniable, as was his scorn for the idle rich. Pressure from the left usually masked an invitation to come over to the good side. Hemingway never completely succumbed to the pressure. This was true even when the communists were sure that he had been converted. Hemingway's own political and aesthetic convictions made him a most unlikely true believer.

The left accused him of lacking meaningful political conviction in an age that urgently required commitment and action. This is simply not true; his political convictions could not be contained within categories drawn by the communists. He denounced Mussolini and Italian fascism almost from the beginning. After an interview with Mussolini in the early 1920s, he described him as a theatrical clown and a bully. After the socialist Matteotti was killed in 1924, he added the epithet murderer. He was among the first to recognize the menace of Hitler and Nazism. In the American election of 1932 he supported the socialist Eugene Debs over both Hoover and Roosevelt.

Hemingway's peculiar amalgam of political ideas, all of American origin, set him against the power ideologies of the twentieth century. To his way of thinking, both fascism and communism stood for violence and the crushing of individual liberty. Beyond that, his political thinking cut across all lines. On different occasions he expressed views ranging from socialist to conservative. Perhaps his political thought is best characterized as in the midwestern populist tradition.

Hemingway was far from naive in political matters. As a reporter and foreign correspondent, he had seen the political process in America and in Europe. He knew the corrupting influence of power, even on many who, out of power, had seemed to be unselfish idealists. He had witnessed revolutions that began with hope and turned to horror. Inevitably, the poor were the ones to suffer. They were forced to shed their blood by misleaders of all ideologies.

Hemingway was a democrat in the Jeffersonian tradition: the less government the better. He repeatedly protested against the taxes that supported the growing bureaucracy in Washington. He scorned the crude efforts of the government to make work for the unemployed at low wages.

When Hemingway contributed an article to the left wing magazine *New Masses*, dealing with the hurricane that drowned many World War I veterans who were working on federal road-building projects in the Florida Keys, it seemed to some that Hemingway was joining the left chorus. They were mistaken. The pressure he felt was coming not so much from the communists as from the actual suffering of Americans in the depression. He blamed the government for the death of the veterans, but as a man and as an artist, he was incapable of submitting to communist ideology or discipline.

On the aesthetic side, Hemingway believed that an artist must remain free to interpret experience without preconceived political guidelines. The artist is not a political propagandist or a writer of textbooks. If a work is to live it must add to the sum of human knowledge, but it is not the cold knowledge of ideology. The artist's political views are implicit in his treatment of everything, including the nonpolitical. If the writer is a servant of anything but truth, his writing will be transitory. Hemingway was right. Most of the "proletarian" literature of the 1930s did not outlive the party line of the decade.

Hemingway returned to the novel with *To Have and Have Not*. Published in 1937, it is based on three short stories he had written around the figure of Harry Morgan, a former police officer in Miami, now making a living as owner and captain of a charter fishing boat in Key West. With the three stories as a core, Hemingway added subplots and additional characters designed to offer a contrast with Harry.

Everything Harry does (he engages in some pretty shady enterprises) originates in his obligation to support his wife, Marie, and their three young daughters. The theme represents a new direction for Hemingway, obviously a reflection of the economic and social realities of the time.

Harry is a strong individual. He has both pity and contempt for the World War I veterans, who accept starvation wages from the government for work on the roads and then cut loose in degrading drunken brawls. Harry's boat is chartered by a wealthy American, a Mr. Johnson, for three weeks of marlin fishing out of Havana. At the end of the three weeks Johnson boards a plane for Florida without bothering to pay Harry. In desperate need of money, Harry contracts to smuggle a boatload of Chinese from Cuba to the United States. Then he turns to smuggling liquor. Finally, he undertakes to transport some Cuban revolutionists from Key West to Cuba.

Harry encounters nothing but trouble from society in the form of decadent people and unfeeling political forces. Johnson swindles him. Harry's arm is amputated after it is severely wounded by a bullet from the Cuban coastguard. An American government bigwig reports his smuggling activities to Key West authorities, who impound his boat.

He borrows a boat from a bartender friend in order to take the revolutionists to Cuba, a venture whose wisdom he doubts, but he needs the money. "I don't want to fool with it but what choice have I got? They don't give you any choice now. I can let it go; but what will the next thing be?"

The revolutionists rob a bank just before they get into Harry's boat. Presumably the money will help finance the revolution. A sadistic brute named Roberto kills Albert, Harry's helper. One of the Cubans tries to explain: "This man Roberto is bad. He is a good revolutionary but a bad man. He kills so much in the time of Machado he gets to like it. He thinks it is funny to kill. He kills in a good cause, of course. The best cause."

In the gun battle that ensues on the boat, all are killed except Harry, who is severely wounded and dies in the Key West hospital. Before the end he manages to say what "it had taken all his life to learn"—"No matter how a man alone ain't got no bloody ——ing chance."

As a positive conclusion, Harry's dying statement does not grow organically from the events of the book. It seems tacked on, forced, surely not the call to mass political action that some leftists thought they saw in it. From the negative side, however, Harry's statement represents what Hemingway was actually driving at. The day of the strong individual is gone. Harry represents the dream, but only the dream, of the self-sufficient individual in American life, Natty Bumppo in a world that has no place for him.

In *To Have and Have Not* Hemingway's awareness of social problems has a significant effect on the character of his hero. Harry is a combination of the sensitive hero whose prototype is Jake Barnes, and the ideal hero whose prototype is Pedro Romero. Harry, though disillusioned, is nonetheless a man of action. His disillusionment does not make him impotent; he acts with courage, with grace under pressure in a losing cause. Hemingway's tragic vision is, by means of the figure of Harry, undergoing a development toward a greater breadth and balance that is continued in the hero of *For Whom the Bell Tolls* and reaches full ripeness in the hero of *The Old Man and the Sea*. Although the development is only suggested in *To Have and Have Not*, the nihilist component of Hemingway's vision will gradually be subordinated to the affirmative component.

Love is central in Hemingway's scheme of things. Harry and Marie enjoy a marriage that has gained in strength over the years. Marie, a big bleached blonde two years older than her husband, seems to be an unlikely candidate for romance, but she possesses many of the attractive features of Catherine Barkley. She is all woman and adores her rough and ready husband. Romantic, sentimental even, she is the heart of the home to which Harry returns for renewal after his dangerous voyages.

In contrast to the loyalty and devotion between Harry and Marie, Hemingway introduces the novelist Richard Gordon and his wife, Helen. Gordon, a successful writer of "proletarian novels," follows the approved communist political formulas—the textile strike, the beautiful female agitator in love with the idealistic strike leader, the rainbow of the future at the close—without infusing any life into them. He writes about things he does not really know. His marriage is as fake as his writing. Contrary to his own high estimate of his amorous talents, he is a failure as husband and lover.

The wealthy slummers in Key West are compared to their detriment with the uneducated men who work for a living and their women who make life livable. The rich are a decadent crew of spineless men, phoneys, nymphomaniacs, and whores.

Hemingway peers into the ships at anchor in the harbor while the boat bearing the mortally wounded Harry is towed into Key West by a Coast Guard cutter. Sketched with economy, the wealthy people are exposed in all their ugliness and decadence. It is a further indictment of the upper strata of American society: a pair of genteel homosexuals have an argument; a ruthless grain broker worries about his imminent indictment on charges of income-tax evasion; the unfaithful wife of an alcoholic movie director cannot fall asleep.

It does not quite come off. *To Have and Have Not* as a total structure is Hemingway's weakest novel. The original stories built around Harry are the soundest part of the book. When Hemingway forces the social and political connotations by introducing and satirizing the wealthy classes, his people verge on caricature. They are never integrated into the central plot line. There is no direct preaching or propaganda; the failure is aesthetic in nature. Yet there are many fine things in the novel. The Hemingway skill in dialogue and description is there, the final paragraph for example:

A large white yacht was coming into the harbor and seven miles out on the horizon you could see a tanker, small and neat in profile against the blue sea, hugging the reef as she made to the westward to keep from wasting fuel against the stream.

Hemingway effectively employs a shifting point of view—now inside Harry, now outside. A modified stream-of-consciousness technique close to the method of the soliloquy takes us into the minds of several characters. Marie's final soliloquy, after Harry's death, is the most successful in the book. She recalls her courtship by Harry, their happy years together, and she prepares to face the future. A new psychological complexity is revealed by Hemingway, foreshadowing the portrayal of Pablo, Pilar, and Anselmo in *For Whom the Bell Tolls.*

The Spanish Civil War broke out in 1936. The monarchy had been overthrown in 1931 and replaced by a Republican government whose efforts at reform were hesitant and inept. As Hemingway saw the situation, a new bureaucracy had taken over, and the money was going into different pockets, but the hard lot of the peasants was only slightly improved. Bothered by the anticlericalism of the Republican government, he nevertheless supported the Republic.

The elections of 1936 resulted in a victory for the Republican parties ranging from the center to the extreme left, including the communists. Large landowners, monarchists, the church, and the military prepared a revolt to overthrow the government by force. Civil war ensued, the fascist rebels aided and abetted by German and Italian arms and men.

In 1937 Hemingway went to Spain as a correspondent for the North American Newspaper Alliance. He hit it off well with the leaders and men of the volunteer international brigades fighting on the Republican side, including the American Abraham Lincoln Brigade, which has become famous in the annals of the American left. They welcomed him and recognized him as a staunch supporter of the Republic of Spain, ready to give freely of his time and money. The communists had been the leaders in organizing the

international brigades and increasingly took over
the planning and direction of the Republican war effort.
Hemingway knew that, but it made no difference in
his antifascist position.

He remained essentially an antifascist as a man and
an artist. A writer, he said at the time, could live under
any kind of government except fascism. He accepted
communist leadership in Spain because the communists
were the best organizers and disciplinarians, and the immediate task was to hold out against the fascists. In no
sense did he commit himself to communism itself.

In 1940, a year after the final victory of Franco,
Hemingway's novel of the Spanish Civil War was published. It was denounced by the communist left as
treachery against the Spanish people and the international brigades. The charges were patently false. Hemingway's support of the Republic and his antifascism
are clear. He refused, however, to write propaganda.
Hemingway's view of the Spanish Civil War strives
for a more complex truth than any streamlined political
program.

The epigraph, which includes the title of *For
Whom the Bell Tolls*, is taken from the *Devotions* of
John Donne:

> No man is an *Iland*, intire of it selfe; every man is a
> peece of the *Continent*, a part of the *maine*; if *Clod* bee
> washed away by the *Sea*, *Europe* is the lesse, as well as if a
> *Promontorie* were, as well as if a *Mannor* of thy *friends*
> or of *thine owne* were; any mans *death* diminishes *me*, be-
> cause I am involved in *Mankinde*; And therefore never
> send to know for whom the *bell* tolls; It tolls for *thee*.

In Donne the passage is a recognition of the one-
ness of all men under God; in Hemingway it means
much the same, with or without God. Some interpreta-

tions have stressed the connection between the epigraph and Hemingway's stand against fascism, a sort of literary reflection of the slogan of collective security. Nothing in the epigraph, however, is at variance with Hemingway's vision of life through *To Have and Have Not*, and that vision is not basically political.

In the novel, Robert Jordan, a young American volunteer with the Republicans, is sent to join a guerrilla band operating in mountainous country behind the fascist lines. His mission is, with the help of the guerrillas, to destroy a bridge so that an impending surprise Republican attack on the city of Segovia will not be jeopardized by prompt enemy reinforcements. In the end, with the bridge successfully destroyed, Jordan, wounded and unable to escape with the surviving guerrillas, waits behind his machine gun to fire on an approaching column of fascist cavalry before he meets his own inevitable death.

Robert Jordan had taken a leave from his position as a Spanish instructor at the University of Montana in order to fight fascism in Spain, a country that he had lived in and which he loved deeply. He accepts the discipline of the communists for the duration of the war because he believes that their discipline is "the soundest and sanest for the prosecution of the war." Jordan has no politics of his own; he senses that when the war is over, he may find himself at odds with communism.

Jordan is a good soldier—intelligent and, when it is required, tough. He is, however, far from becoming the Roberto of *To Have and Have Not*. Killing is wrong, and only the possibility of greater wrong can justify it: "You mustn't believe in killing, he told himself. You must do it as a necessity but you must not believe in it. If you believe in it the whole thing is wrong." Jordan is Frederic Henry fighting a war whose purposes he believes in.

Jordan's family background parallels Hemingway's own in several important respects. Ed Hemingway had killed himself with his father's Civil War revolver; Jordan's father had killed himself in the same way. "Usually his [Jordan's] mind was very good company and tonight it had been when he thought about his grandfather. Then thinking of his father had thrown him off. He understood his father and he forgave him everything and he pitied him but he was ashamed of him."

The members of the guerrilla band are individualized to a degree that Hemingway never attempted previously with so many characters. It is as though Hemingway, in portraying his beloved Spanish people, is emotionally impelled to come closer to them. He not only tells us what they do and say; he tries to explain them, each one, as whole human beings. He is most successful with Pablo, Pilar, and Anselmo.

Pablo, the leader of the band, is a tough, wily man whose will to fight has slackened with the increasing comfort of the mountain cave in which they live and with the acquisition of property in the form of captured horses. He looks upon Jordan as a threat to his security; the task of blowing up the bridge, even if successful, will expose them to attack by the fascists. The cave will no longer be a haven of refuge, and they will be compelled to move to another region for a new start. He comes to understand, even to admire the intelligence, skill, and courage of Jordan, but he opposes his mission. Brought to the breaking point, he defects, taking with him some of Jordan's dynamiting equipment. Unable, however, to live with his aloneness and treachery he rejoins the band at the critical juncture

and fights ferociously against the fascist reinforcements. He is a complex man.

Pilar, Pablo's woman, a unity of conflicting quali-
ties—overflowing with the joy of life, tougher than
Pablo himself, completely dedicated to the Republican
cause, capable of the greatest refinement of feeling—
knows that Pablo is no longer trustworthy. She assumes
the leadership of the band in cooperation with Jordan,
with whom she develops a mother-son relationship.

The wonderful old man, Anselmo, is drawn in the
warmest colors. If anyone in the book may be said to
speak for Hemingway, it is Anselmo. He becomes Jordan's special assistant in the dynamiting of the bridge.
Rugged, always dependable, he and Jordan have a relationship that must be described in terms of love. They sit
and talk of the war, God, killing, all the big questions.
The old man is even more averse to killing than Jordan
and does so only in a torment of soul. His logic is very
much like Jordan's, but his struggle is greater because
emotionally he must overcome an almost saintly feeling
for human life. He is a hunter and has no hesitation in
killing animals. He discusses hunting with Jordan:

> "You like to hunt?"
> "No," said Robert Jordan. "I do not like to kill ani-
> mals."
> "With me it is the opposite," the old man said. "I do
> not like to kill men."
> "Nobody does except those who are disturbed in the
> head," Robert Jordan said.

Anselmo says that it is a sin to kill a man, even a
fascist. He has killed fascists and knows that he will kill
again, but he refuses to take himself off the hook. He
will do what must be done but without talking himself
into self-righteousness. Later he will need forgiveness

from himself, not from God in whom he no longer believes. He tells Jordan: "With or without God, I think
it is a sin to kill. To take the life of another is to me very
grave. I will do it whenever necessary but I am not of
the race of Pablo."

The band, during an attack on a train some months
before Jordan's arrival, has rescued Maria, the daughter
of antifascist parents who had been executed by the
fascists. Raped by the fascist soldiers, her head shaved,
she was out of her mind when the band found her. Pilar
nurses her back to something approaching health. Jordan and Maria become lovers, with the blessing of Pilar.
Their love marks the return of Maria to full health and
life.

Maria does not come through with the clear definition of the others. She is the Hemingway woman, living
to serve the physical and emotional needs of her man,
romanticized beyond anything in the earlier novels. The
love scenes in the sleeping bag have become famous.
The sexual relationship between Jordan and Maria is
ecstatic: when they make love, "the earth moves."
When Jordan, wounded so that he cannot escape with
the guerrillas, tries to convince Maria that she must go
with them, he tells her that they will always be one:
"If thou goest then I go with thee. It is in that way that
I go too. Thou wilt go now, I know. For thou art good
and kind. Thou wilt go now for us both."

No fair-minded reader can doubt that *For Whom
the Bell Tolls* is an antifascist novel. It is clear, however,
that Hemingway's treatment of the war as a whole aims
at the kind of truth that extends beyond politics. The
book contains many complexities and ambiguities that
lift its stature as an aesthetic achievement but that were
the basis for leftist anger.

The Republicans are inefficient and lacking in dis-

cipline. The planned attack on Segovia is known to the
fascists, as Jordan realizes when large formations of
German and Italian planes are sighted flying toward
that city. When he sends one of the guerrillas with a
dispatch to General Golz advising that the attack be
called off, the messenger is detained long enough to
prevent appropriate action because of the megalomania
and stupidity of André Marty, the French organizer of
the international brigades.

Hemingway attacks several of the communist "heroes" of the Spanish Civil War. He does not always
show the Russian volunteers and advisers in a favorable
light. Even his beloved Spanish people are revealed as
the best and worst of mankind.

In the entire book there is nothing so shocking as
Pilar's detailed account of the horrors inflicted in her
town on the fascists and their sympathizers by the
Republicans at the outset of the civil war. It is men-
tioned that even more horrible things were done by the
fascists when they retook the town. The fact remains,
however, that it is Pilar's account that sticks in the
reader's mind.

Hemingway was in a real sense two men when he
wrote *For Whom the Bell Tolls*. One man was sup-
porting the war against forces whose victory would
engulf the entire world in a greater war. This man saw
the fascist planes as "mechanized doom." The other
man had seen the horror and hollowness of war in Italy
while he was still a young man. He never got over it.
His opposition to war, any war, was based on a human-
itarian rather than a political insight. The easy leftist
distinction between good and bad wars could not, in
the deepest recesses of his being, be accepted as the
whole truth. Fascists are not all beasts; antifascists are
not all angels.

Stylistically, *For Whom the Bell Tolls* shows Hemingway moving toward greater linguistic freedom and innovation. The writing is less laconic than before, yet the fundamental economy of language remains. The words still convey much more than the dictionary meanings, yet Hemingway tells the reader more, explains more. He attempts, by and large successfully, to catch the flavor of the Spanish language by use of "thee" and "thou" and by imitating the idiomatic inversions of the peasant usage.

Finally, the book contains one of the great battle scenes in literature, worthy of rank with the retreat from Caporetto in *A Farewell to Arms*—that is, the destruction by air attack of the guerrilla band led by El Sordo and trapped on a mountaintop by a fascist cavalry patrol.

8

○○○

Growing
Old

Not until 1950, ten years after *For Whom the Bell Tolls*, was a new Hemingway novel published, *Across the River and Into the Trees*, and then it was a disappointment to both the critics and general readers. Many said that Hemingway had simply exhausted himself and that he had nothing more to say. There is little doubt that in the 1940s Hemingway was finding it increasingly difficult to sustain the creative pitch necessary for writing major fiction. Even the short stories that he continued to turn out were not up to his earlier work. The virility and compassion of his best stories were changing to cheap heroics and sentimentality. The old firm control over his material seemed to be collapsing.

Some critics spotlighted Hemingway's personal life as the source of his artistic difficulties. Amateur and professional psychiatrists analyzed his psyche in public. During the 1940s Hemingway was in all respects a public figure. He was not only recognized as America's foremost novelist; his reputation as a war correspondent, as a man's man, made him good copy. Wherever the action was, there was Hemingway. When the United States entered World War II, Hemingway, operating from his fishing boat, the *Pilar*, organized his own antisubmarine and antiespionage patrol in the Caribbean. It never accomplished much, had its comicopera aspects, and the best that can be said for it is that it did no permanent injury to Hemingway, the war effort, or the German submarines.

As a war correspondent, he was in on the invasion of Normandy by the Allies, flew on several bombing missions, participated in the taking of Paris, and was in the thick of the fighting in the Hurtgen Forest, through it all making new friends and consolidating old enmities. He was tried and acquitted by the military on charges of organizing a partisan group and engaging in combat activities forbidden to correspondents. After the hubbub subsided, he was awarded a decoration in recognition of his efforts.

In 1940 Hemingway purchased a house in the village of San Francisco de Paula, about fifteen miles from Havana. It became his home for almost twenty years, until political upheavals soured him on Cuba. In 1939 he took his first trip to Sun Valley, located near the town of Ketchum, Idaho. He returned there regularly for hunting, fishing, and rest, and in 1959 bought a house there.

In 1940, several months after his second marriage ended in divorce, Hemingway married Martha Gellhorn, a young journalist. Five years later, this marriage, too, ended in divorce. In 1946 he married his fourth wife, Mary Welch, whom he met in London during the war. It turned out to be a happy marriage, which lasted until Hemingway's death fifteen years later.

In 1948 Hemingway took a trip to Italy for the first time since 1927. Making Venice, a city that he loved deeply, his base of operations, he and Mary made short trips into northern Italy and one to the scene of his 1918 war experiences. In Venice he was friendly with several members of the Italian aristocracy, particularly a girl of nineteen named Adriana Ivancich. Out of this visit to Italy grew *Across the River and Into the Trees*.

The title is a shortened version of Stonewall Jackson's words after he was mortally wounded at Chancellorsville. He requested of his officers that they should cross the river so that he might rest in the shade of the trees. Jackson died in the shade of those trees, and that is the point of reference for Hemingway. His book has the elegiac tone of a man awaiting death. The central figure is Colonel Richard Cantwell, on duty with the American forces in Italy after World War II. He takes a vacation trip to his beloved Venice to see his young Italian mistress, Renata—the name means reborn—and to do some duck shooting.

Richard Cantwell is a career soldier of fifty in the American infantry. He has fought in both great wars of the twentieth century, as a young officer with the Italian army in World War I, in his maturity with the American army in France and Germany in World War II.

This is a story of a man becoming aware that he is on the threshold of old age. He will not, however, meekly turn his back on a life that he loves and whose compensations he has learned to appreciate with delicate sensibility. He knows that his diseased heart may decide to quit at any moment. His body is scarred with wounds sustained in his trade. The desire for life, however, remains stronger than ever. He tenaciously holds onto his total personality, that is, his contradictory makeup: tough, gentle, truculent, cultured, egotistical, honest. Without distortion or self-justification, he continually evaluates his life.

Although Hemingway drew on several American officers whom he had met in World War II for his portrait of Cantwell—especially General Lanham, with whose division he had covered the attack on the German Westwall—it is clear that in many respects Cantwell is an alter ego of the author. Cantwell emerges as a combination of Hemingway and his fictional heroes grown old. It is hard to resist the impression that in this book Hemingway is rethinking his own values, literary and nonliterary. Sometimes the protagonist seems to step forward as Hemingway rather than Cantwell. For example, in a dinner conversation between Cantwell

and Renata, the subject comes around to the relationship between writing and the moral nature of the
writer:

"You don't know how important things that are said
are."

"They are a damn sight more important when you put
them on paper."

"No," the girl said. "I don't agree. The paper means
nothing unless you say them in your heart."

"And what if you haven't a heart, or your heart is
worthless?"

"You have a heart and it is not worthless."

Cantwell makes a pilgrimage to Fossalta, where he
had been wounded in World War I (Hemingway himself had been wounded there in World War I). There
he writes finis to the traumatic experience by perform-
ing a ritual act of defecation in the exact place where
he had been when the shell exploded.

Cantwell has made a cult of the military brotherhood. His heart goes out to all soldiers who have seen
combat, even more to infantrymen, and most to men
who were wounded in action: "He only loved people,
he thought, who had fought or been mutilated. Other
people were fine and you liked them and were good
friends; but you only felt true tenderness and love for
those who had been there and had received the casti-
gation that everyone receives who goes there long
enough."

He is trigger-quick to use his fists when he feels
slighted or insulted in any way. He challenges two
fascists who are discussing him under the assumption
that he does not understand Italian. He flattens two
American sailors who whistle at the attractive Renata.
On the other hand, he is quite capable of criticizing,
not without a gentle pathos, his compulsive aggressive-

ness: "Why am I always a bastard and why can I not
suspend this trade of arms, and be a kind and good man
as I would have wished to be. I try always to be just,
but I am brusque and brutal. I should be a better man
with less wild boar blood in the small time which remains."

The recurrent strain of *Across the River and Into
the Trees* is the issue of death. How does one die?
There is considerable rumination on graves and putre-
faction. The theme is not new in Hemingway's work,
and in this book it is central. As Hemingway sees it,
however, the question of death is really the question of
life. How does a worthy man live?

The answer for Hemingway is not a negation.
True, a man would be a fool not to acknowledge the
cruelty and corruption of the human race and the
capriciousness of events, but it is necessary to be a
stoic. A man must believe that all is not wrong with the
universe even though he cannot fit together all the
pieces. Cantwell does not succumb to disillusionment
with mankind. The sacredness of the heart's affections
is assumed in Hemingway's art.

On the whole, *Across the River and Into the Trees*
represents a falling off; it is not one of Hemingway's
major novels. The portrait of Renata is perhaps the
weakest element. She does not come through as a real-
ized figure. Whatever reality she has comes through
Cantwell's view of her: she is his last true love, his
dream of youth and of the ideal. The love scenes are
self-conscious to the point of seeming to be posed. The
conversations between Cantwell and Renata are sometimes cuddly-coy. It is Hemingway imitating himself
rather than being himself. He seems to be in doubt
about the validity of the emotions attributed to his
lovers.

In Hemingway's best work the symbols arise unobtrusively out of people and situations so that, in a formal sense, they are not symbols at all. In this book, however, the symbolism is vitiated by mannerism in the foreground. For once the foreground failed Hemingway; the things close to the reader's eye do not seem real enough or honest enough. Rather than feeling their emotions, Cantwell and Renata tell each other what their emotions should be. Cantwell is given the job of explaining the symbolism of the book. It does not work.

The formal structure of the book, however, is new for Hemingway and is highly successful. When the curtain rises Cantwell is going to a duck-shoot, and in the end we are returned to it. All that is in between is essentially Cantwell's reliving of his holiday with Renata. The descriptive passages dealing with the bridges, canals, and buildings of Venice, the ocean, and the countryside are among the best Hemingway ever wrote. *Across the River and Into the Trees* represents an artistic decline, but it is still the work of a master.

9

○○○○○○○○○○○○○○○○○○○○○○○○○○○○○○○○ ○○○○○○○○○○○○○○○○

Lions
on the
Beach

In 1952, only two years after the cool reception accorded to *Across the River and Into the Trees, The Old Man and the Sea* was greeted with critical acclaim as Hemingway's return to full power. It won him the Pulitzer Prize for 1952.

The shortest of Hemingway's novels, *The Old Man and the Sea* might properly be classified as a novella. The structure and texture of the book are based on a single uncomplicated incident in the life of an old Cuban fisherman named Santiago. Only the old man, with the possible addition of his young admirer, Manolo, is characterized in depth. The plot of *The Old Man and the Sea* had been revolving in Hemingway's mind since 1936. Now, viewing himself as an old man, Hemingway discovered new riches in the story of the old fisherman.

Santiago has not caught a fish for eighty-four days. On this day, hoping that his luck will turn, he rows his skiff out of the Havana harbor before the sun is up. His intention is to fish the waters farther out than he has ever done, far beyond the area fished by other fishermen. He is looking for "the big one," the fish that will not only pay him well but will restore his pride as a man. He hooks a gigantic marlin that makes a run for the open sea to the north and east, pulling the skiff. The fish does not come to the surface; only from the swift movement of the boat does Santiago know what kind of fish he has hooked. After two days, the marlin surfaces and leaps clear of the water in his efforts to throw the hook. On the third day the fish, tiring, begins to circle the skiff; Santiago is able to pull the fish closer to the boat. Finally alongside the skiff, the fish is harpooned and killed. Since he is longer than the boat, the marlin must be lashed to the gunwales for the return trip to Havana. Then the sharks come, singly and in packs, and despite the efforts of the old man, they tear the flesh from the marlin's body. Only the skeleton remains when the skiff is secured on shore. The old man, shouldering the mast with the sail furled around it, staggers to his cabin and goes to sleep.

In discussing *The Old Man and the Sea*, again the worst approach is to read Hemingway directly into Santiago. Along that road the sharks may become Hemingway's critics and the entire book an exercise in self-justification and self-pity. To recognize, however, that Santiago is part of Hemingway's spiritual history, is another matter. The story of the old fisherman reflects Hemingway's mature tragic vision.

The Old Man and the Sea is Hemingway's clearest tragic assertion. Fully acknowledging the presence of evil and the vagaries of circumstances, Hemingway nevertheless pays homage to the raw energy of the universe and the fundamental partnership between man and nature. Although Santiago wants to kill the fish, he feels admiration for it, a bond of love and respect between worthy antagonists. The struggle between man and fish is a fair contest calling up the spectator's wonder and compassion. When the sharks attack, an active principle of evil intrudes, and Santiago must apologize to the fish. "I'm sorry about it, fish. It makes everything wrong." Perhaps not quite everything. The fish and the man have played it honorably, but there is more to the world than that. The antagonists are losers together, but also winners together.

The principle of evil in the book is based on Hemingway's impressionistic feeling rather than on a reasoned philosophy. The Portuguese man of war, a creature that floats on the water by means of a gelatinous bladder, trailing deadly filaments behind, Santiago calls a whore. The shark is also evil. The evil is that which is mean, cowardly, ungallant, selfish, or cruel. Santiago, after the mutilation of his marlin, expresses his doubts, however, about the lone Mako shark that made the first attack: "He [the Mako] lives on the live fish as you do. He is not a scavenger nor just a moving appetite as some sharks are. He is beautiful and noble and knows no fear of anything." Perhaps this shark was, in some respects, like the fisherman; evil alone cannot account for the frustrations of men.

The Old Man and the Sea has often been characterized as a parable, that is, a short fiction that expresses or implies a moral or religious principle. Jesus, as recorded by the Gospels, usually delivered his moral preachments in the form of parables, stripped of all elaboration. Stylistically, perhaps, Hemingway's book bears the closest resemblance to the biblical parable. Hemingway extends his habitual economy of diction into an economy of structure and treatment. Peripheral matters are pared to the bone. Santiago's physical appearance is sketched rather than painted; the other characters are merely outlined, usually not even given a name.

Santiago, battling the huge fish, is a lone man on the sea. Yet his connections with humanity and history reach back to the land. First, there is the boy, Manolo, who has been forbidden by his parents to sail with Santiago because they fear that the old man's bad luck may rub off on the boy. At the end the boy resolves to rejoin his mentor. As the battered old man prepares to rest after his labors, the boy says to him: "You must get well fast for there is much that I can learn and you can teach me everything." The boy, who brings food and medicine to Santiago, never loses faith in Santiago's stature as a fisherman and hero.

It is usual for Hemingway's heroes to be loved, even venerated. In the other novels, it is a woman who loves the hero; here, it is a boy who loves him. Hemingway grows old, but one might say more. The tie that binds Manolo to Santiago is the linking of the generations and the hope of continuing life, the need of the old for the young and the young for the old.

The old man had been happily married; his wife is dead. On the walls of his shack "was a picture in color of the Sacred Heart of Jesus and another of the Virgin of Cobre. These were relics of his wife. Once there had been a tinted photograph of his wife on the wall but he had taken it down because it made him too lonely to see it and it was on the shelf in the corner under his clean shirt."

Santiago has his connections with the past, his own history. In his youth he had been strong, a champion. In an epic arm-wrestling match he had put down a challenger of fabulous might. Now the old man dreams of lions on African beaches that he had seen long ago from the deck of a square rigged ship. The boy sits open-mouthed as the old man tells him of the dream. As the prophet Joel says, "Your old men shall dream dreams, your young men shall see visions."

The "lions on the beach" have been variously interpreted. The reader may permit himself the widest latitude without going wrong or doing violence to the words—a dream of adventure, of boundless energy and pride, of love for the universe, of the million bounties of life. It is a phrase whose general meaning is clear but in which each man may find something special for himself.

When, his ordeal over, the old man lies down on his bed, it is as Christ crucified: "He pulled the blanket over his shoulders and then over his back and legs and he slept face down on the newspapers with his arms out straight and the palms of his hands up."

One may wonder whether the Christ image is entirely appropriate. It would appear that it reinforces the thrust of the book if Christ is conceived in his human aspect only. The *suffering* Christ is consistent with Hemingway's tragic vision. Santiago is the son of man, not of God. Although he calls on God and prays several times during his struggle with the marlin, he explicitly states that he is no believer. On this issue, Santiago mirrors Hemingway's own will to believe without ever being able to attain consummation in God. As a tragic figure the old fisherman is best left to his own resources. When he says that he "shouldn't have gone out so far" we should not take him at his word. The next time he will go out even farther.

The Old Man and the Sea may not be Hemingway's greatest novel but it is the one in which his mature and balanced vision of the human condition received its finest expression.

10

○○○○○○○○○○○○○○○○○○○○○○○○○○○○○○○○ ○○○○○○○○○○○○○○○

Memories
and
Decline

The Old Man and the Sea was Hemingway's last major work of fiction. In the remaining nine years of his life he fought an inevitably losing battle against illness, old age, and the general decline of his creative energy. Several novels were projected and begun but none were completed. The short stories written during the last decade of his life do not compare favorably with the masterpieces of the 1920s and 1930s in the same genre. He continued to write for magazines, particularly about a new hunting expedition to Africa and about the rivalry between the best of the new generation of bullfighters, Antonio Ordoñez and Luis Miguel Dominguin.

The African safari with Mary in 1953 and 1954 gave Hemingway great pleasure. Philip Percival, his much admired guide twenty years earlier, came out of retirement to lead the party. Hemingway seemed to recapture the vitality and enthusiasm of his younger days. The finale, however, was disastrous: two successive airplane crashes in Uganda at the end of the trip almost killed Hemingway and his wife. In fact, his death was reported in many newspapers. Hereafter, his health was poor; he suffered from hypertension, a serious liver disorder, and numerous other ailments occasioned by the airplane crashes and a lifetime of accidents that had left him beaten and scarred. He always insisted that he was not accident-prone. However that may have been, his scars were proof of many accidents over his lifetime.

He struggled to regain his health; the doctors prescribed vitamins, forbade alcohol, and put him on a strict diet. For a man as full of *joie de vivre* as Hemingway was, the restrictions were irksome. He lapsed into periods of depression that became more severe as he grew older.

In 1953 he was awarded the Nobel Prize, "the Swedish thing" as he called it. He felt it was long overdue and he had perhaps despaired of ever being so recognized. Since the established rule called for the Nobel Prize to be awarded for writing "of ideal tendencies," Hemingway's fiction, whether justly or unjustly, might be considered inappropriate. *The Old Man and the Sea* apparently was decisive in the thinking of the prize committee. The citation called attention to Hemingway's "natural admiration for every individual who fights the good fight in a world of reality overshadowed by violence and death." Specific reference to the earlier writings, however, passed judgment upon them as "brutal, cynical and callous." The committee would seem to have succumbed to the prevalent misreading of Hemingway's works.

Hemingway's health did not allow him to accept the prize in person. He recorded and sent a simple, modest statement without flourishes.

Between 1957 and 1960, Hemingway worked intermittently on writing down his reminiscences of the years in Paris from 1921 to 1926. Under the title *A Moveable Feast*, the sketches were published in 1964, three years after his death. In its entirety *A Moveable Feast* recaptures the happiness of the young Hemingway with his new career as a writer, with Paris, with his marriage. The sheer joy of life in Paris is re-created, the excitement of the blood that went with the sidewalk cafés, the paintings, and parks. The Paris of his learning years had always remained vivid in his mind, "a moveable feast" as he termed it.

The book deals with the famous literary personalities whom Hemingway had met in Paris. First, there is the settling of accounts with Gertrude Stein, and to a lesser extent, with Ford Madox Ford. He tells it as he recalls it. Not unexpectedly, Gertrude Stein does not come off very well in his account of their relationship. Although many things are revealed that must come under the heading of literary gossip, on the whole it seems that Hemingway is closer to the significant truth than is Gertrude Stein in her account: his literary success owed little to her influence and teaching. More in the comic vein is the deflation of Ford Madox Ford, whose literary association with Hemingway in the 1920s had not been too rewarding for either of them.

In one of the sketches Hemingway blames his second wife, Pauline, and her money for the breakup of his first marriage. From the distance of thirty odd years he manages to absolve himself of any serious share in the blame.

Ezra Pound is portrayed with warm affection. In Hemingway's view Pound was a great poet and a kind, generous man. Eccentric, never quite grown up, he could always be counted on to help budding writers in need of literary guidance or of material assistance. Without any thought of self-aggrandizement, he took upon himself the responsibility for the literary and political health of the universe.

Hemingway considered Scott Fitzgerald, sober, the most loyal friend he had; he also considered him a weak, unstable human being. Concerning the strange marital relationship of the Fitzgeralds, Hemingway bluntly declares his belief that it was Zelda who ruined her husband's first-rate literary talent. She looked upon Scott's writing as her chief rival and tormented him into doubting his own ability as writer and man. His heavy drinking and general dissipation were encouraged by Zelda. As Hemingway saw it, not until Zelda was judged definitely insane did Fitzgerald return to serious writing, and by then he was far gone.

Among the most valuable portions of *A Moveable Feast* are Hemingway's reflections on his own development as an artist. He tells, for instance, of his "new theory that you could omit anything if you knew that you omitted and the omitted part would strengthen the story and make people feel something more than they understood." The passage is of prime importance, since the effect described is precisely what Hemingway achieves in his best fiction—a suspension of the need for full rational explanation of people and events. Hemingway implicitly recognizes that in experience there is much that remains obscure and ambiguous, and that an honest rendition of experience does not necessarily explain everything. In Hemingway's fiction, the truth is often of the human heart at war with itself.

The last two years of Hemingway's life were marked by an unmistakable deterioration of body and mind. He lost weight; his blood pressure was dangerously high. His once infallible memory failed him; he could not accurately recall the events on which he had always drawn for his writing. Most ominous, he suffered increasingly severe periods of nervous depression. In 1960 he showed suicidal tendencies and entered the Mayo Clinic in Minnesota for treatment. Released in 1961, he returned to Ketchum, only to go back to the Mayo Clinic a few months later. He was released again, in spite of the misgivings of his wife. Hemingway committed suicide in the house at Ketchum by shooting himself with a double-barreled shotgun on 2 July 1961.

The Nobel Prize citation had paid its highest respects to Hemingway for "his powerful, style-making mastery of the art of modern narration." The Hemingway style was considered the most influential aspect of his writing during his lifetime. The substance, or what was thought to be the substance of his writing, was relegated to a secondary position. Hemingway himself always felt that the critics did not see in his fiction all there was to see. In his recorded speech of acceptance to the Nobel Prize committee he said that "things may not be immediately discernible in what a man writes, and in this sometimes he is fortunate; but eventually they are quite clear and by these and the degree of alchemy that he possesses he will endure or be forgotten."

It is likely that in this statement Hemingway was criticizing the citation as well as the critics. Undoubtedly Hemingway will endure partly because of his style, his alchemy, as he terms it. One must ponder, however, the possibility that what Hemingway has written still remains, in a sense, to be read for the first time. It may be that eventually the hidden and the overlooked in his work will become "quite clear," as he says. The surface of his fiction was immediately impressive. The positive, humanistic core of his fiction—tentative, held in check by his toughness and his style—has not been fully explored or appreciated. Hemingway revealed the spiritual conflicts and dilemmas of his age, and, to a degree, of all ages. Perhaps Hemingway achieved something far more difficult than writers in earlier centuries had been faced with. In an age of spiritual decay and defeat, presenting honestly the condition of that age, he yet upheld the goodness, nobility, and spiritual worth of mankind.

Hemingway disliked rhetoric. He seems to have disliked Faulkner's passionate Nobel Prize statement of the writer's function. Yet it is more than possible that Hemingway himself will ultimately be judged as having lived up to what Faulkner asked of the writer:

He must teach himself that the basest of all things is to be afraid; and, teaching himself that, forget it forever, leaving no room in his workshop for anything but the old verities and truths of the heart, the old universal truths lacking which any story is ephemeral and doomed—love and honor and pity and pride and compassion and sacrifice.

Bibliography

1. Works by Ernest Hemingway

Three Stories and Ten Poems. Paris: Contact, 1923.

in our time. Paris: Three Mountains, 1924.

In Our Time. New York: Boni and Liveright, 1925.

The Torrents of Spring. New York: Scribner's, 1926.

The Sun Also Rises. New York: Scribner's, 1926.

Men without Women. New York: Scribner's, 1927.

A Farewell to Arms. New York: Scribner's, 1929.

Death in the Afternoon. New York: Scribner's, 1932.

Winner Take Nothing. New York: Scribner's, 1933.

Green Hills of Africa. New York: Scribner's, 1935.

To Have and Have Not. New York: Scribner's, 1937.

The Fifth Column, and The First Forty-nine Stories. New York: Scribner's, 1938.

For Whom the Bell Tolls. New York: Scribner's, 1940.

Men at War. Edited and with an introduction by Hemingway. New York: Crown, 1942.

Across the River and Into the Trees. New York: Scribner's, 1950.

The Old Man and the Sea. New York: Scribner's, 1952.

A Moveable Feast. New York: Scribner's, 1964.

Islands in the Stream. New York: Scribner's, 1972.

The Nick Adams Stories. Preface by Philip Young. New York: Scribner's, 1972.

2. *Works about Ernest Hemingway*

Aldridge, John W. *After the Lost Generation: A Critical Study of the Writers of Two Wars.* New York: Mc-Graw-Hill, 1951.

Algren, Nelson. *Notes from a Sea Diary: Hemingway All the Way.* New York: Putnam, 1965.

Asselineau, Roger, ed. *The Literary Reputation of Hemingway in Europe.* New York: New York University Press, 1965.

Astre, G. A. *Hemingway par lui-même.* Paris: Editions du Seuil, 1959.

Atkins, John. *The Art of Ernest Hemingway: His Work and Personality.* London: Peter Nevill, 1952.

Baker, Carlos. *Hemingway: The Writer as Artist.* Princeton: Princeton University Press, 1952.

———. *Ernest Hemingway: A Life Story.* New York: Scribner's, 1969.

———, ed. *Hemingway and His Critics: An International Anthology.* New York: Hill and Wang, 1961.

Beach, Joseph Warren. *American Fiction: 1920–1940.* New York: Macmillan, 1941.

Benson, Jackson J. *Hemingway: The Writer's Art of Self-Defense.* Minneapolis: University of Minnesota Press, 1969.

Cowley, Malcolm, ed. *After the Genteel Tradition: American Writers since 1910.* New York: W. W. Norton, 1937.

Fenton, Charles A. *The Apprenticeship of Ernest Hemingway*. New York: Farrar, Straus and Young, 1954.

Geismar, Maxwell. *Writers in Crisis: The American Novel between Two Wars*. Boston: Houghton Mifflin, 1942.

Gurko, Leo. *Ernest Hemingway and the Pursuit of Heroism*. New York: Crowell, 1968.

Hemingway, Leicester. *My Brother, Ernest Hemingway*. Cleveland: World, 1962.

Hoffman, Frederick J. *The Modern Novel in America: 1900–1950*. Chicago: Regnery, 1951.

Hotchner, A. E. *Papa Hemingway: A Personal Memoir*. New York: Random House, 1966.

Kazin, Alfred. *On Native Grounds: An Interpretation of Modern American Prose Literature*. New York: Harcourt, Brace, 1942.

Killinger, John. *Hemingway and the Dead Gods: A Study in Existentialism*. Lexington: University of Kentucky Press, 1960.

Loeb, Harold. *The Way It Was*. New York: Criterion, 1959.

McCaffery, John K. M., ed. *Ernest Hemingway: The Man and His Work*. New York: World, 1950.

Montgomery, Constance Cappel. *Hemingway in Michigan*. New York: Fleet, 1966.

Ross, Lillian. *Portrait of Hemingway*. New York: Simon and Schuster, 1961.

Sanderson, Stewart F. *Ernest Hemingway*. London: Oliver and Boyd, 1961.

Sanford, Marcelline Hemingway. *At the Hemingways: A Family Portrait*. Boston: Atlantic-Little, Brown, 1962.

Young, Philip. *Ernest Hemingway*. New York: Rinehart, 1952.

Index